MOVIE MANIA!

Movie-goers, here's your ticket to box-office bonanza on the trivia scene. With this book as your script, your answers will be right on cue!

Here's a sneak preview of coming attractions:

—Who played Garp's mother in THE WORLD AC-CORDING TO GARP?
—Who played Jack Lemmon's henchman sidekick in THE GREAT RACE?
—Who supplied the voice of Darth Vadar in the STAR WARS trilogy?
—Frances Gumm was what famous actress's real name?
—Which distinguished composer won the Oscar for the musical score of THE HEIRESS?
—What city was the background for THE VERDICT?
—Who played Superman's mother in SUPERMAN?
—Who played the sensual female lead in THE NIGHT PORTER?
—Who sang the title song to the James Bond movie OCTOPUSSY?
—Which actress has won the most Best Actress Oscars?

For the answers to these and a thousand others, keep on reading and become the celluloid superstar of TRIVIA MANIA!

TRIVIA MANIA
by Xavier Einstein

TRIVIA MANIA has arrived! With enough questions to answer every trivia buff's dreams, TRIVIA MANIA covers it all—from the delightfully obscure to the <u>seemingly obvious</u>. Tickle your fancy, and test your memory!

MOVIES

TRIVIA Mania

XAVIER EINSTEIN

originated by Charles Steven Cohen

ZEBRA BOOKS
KENSINGTON PUBLISHING CORP.

For my wife, Alexandra — love Charles

ZEBRA BOOKS

are published by

Kensington Publishing Corp.
475 Park Avenue South
New York, N.Y. 10016

First printing: June, 1984

Printed in the United States of America

TRIVIA MANIA:
Movies

1) What film won the 1983 Academy Award for Best Picture?

2) Who won the 1983 Oscar for Best Supporting Actress?

3) *The Big Chill* won an Oscar for Best Screenplay written directly for the screen. True or False?

4) At the 1983 Academy Awards, what was named Best Original Song?

5) What was the name of the high school in *Grease?*
    a. Beaumont High
    b. Harrison High
    c. Presley High
    d. Rydell High
    e. Montgomery High

6) Who played the female lead in *High Road to China?*

. . . Answers

1. *Terms of Endearment*

2. Linda Hunt

3. False (*Tender Mercies*)

4. "Flashdance . . . What a Feeling"

5. (d)

6. Bess Armstrong

QUESTIONS

7) What actor portrayed the role of an American private investigator in *The Yakuza?*

8) Who directed the 1958 screen version of *Rally 'Round the Flag Boys!?*

9) Detective Mike Hammer was portrayed by what actor in the 1958 film, *Kiss Me Deadly?*

10) Diane Keaton had a starring role in Woody Allen's *A Midsummer Night's Sex Comedy.* True or False?

11) Actors Ryan O'Neal and _____ played the title roles in *Partners.*

12) Ed Sullivan played himself in the film musical entitled . . .
    a. *How to Succeed in Business Without Really Trying*
    b. *A Funny Thing Happened on the Way to the Forum*
    c. *On the Town*
    d. *The Toast of the Town*
    e. *Bye, Bye, Birdie*

13) Who played the role of Sheriff Buford Pusser in the 1973 film, *Walking Tall?*

14) In *Body Heat,* who played the role of the arsonist?

15) *A Boy Named Charlie Brown* featured songs written by _____.

. . . Answers

7. Robert Mitchum

8. Leo McCarey

9. Ralph Meeker

10. False

11. John Hurt

12. (e)

13. Joe Don Baker

14. Mickey Rourke

15. Rod McKuen

16) Who portrayed Helen Morgan in *The Helen Morgan Story?*

17) Who played the part of Jay Gatsby in the 1949 film version of *The Great Gatsby?*

18) The voluptuous twins in *Cobra Woman* (1944) were played by what actress?

19) What was the name of Han Solo's spaceship in *Star Wars?*

20) Susannah York played the female lead in Robert Altman's *Images*. True or False?

21) Sidney Poitier and Sammy Davis, Jr. both had leading roles in . . .
    a. *Uptown Saturday Night*
    b. *Robin and the Seven Hoods*
    c. *Porgy and Bess*
    d. *Lilies of the Field*
    e. *In the Heat of the Night*

22) Mervyn LeRoy directed *The Wizard of Oz*. True or False?

23) What well-known American actor made his screen debut in *The Silver Chalice?*

24) Marlon Brando and _____ played the male leads in *Bedtime Story.*

. . . Answers

16. Ann Blyth

17. Alan Ladd

18. Maria Montez

19. Millenium Falcon

20. True

21. (c)

22. False (Victor Fleming)

23. Paul Newman

24. David Niven

25) Who played the female lead in the western, *100 Rifles?*

26) The role of Max Herschel in *Just Tell me What You Want* was played by what actor?

27) Who played the role of Adam in John Huston's screen version of *The Bible?*

28) Who played Anne Frank in the film of *The Diary of Anne Frank?*

29) Who played the female lead opposite Rock Hudson in *Man's Favorite Sport?*

30) Alec Guiness portrayed the murderous hero intent upon eliminating the entire D'Ascoyne family in *Kind Hearts and Coronets.* True or False?

31) Who played the male lead in the film version of *Black Like Me?*

32) The female lead in Chaplin's *Modern Times* was played by actress _____.

33) Michael York and Marisa Berenson both had supporting roles in . . .
    a. *An American in Paris*
    b. *The Three Musketeers*
    c. *All That Jazz*
    d. *Barry Lyndon*
    e. *Cabaret*

. . . Answers

25. Raquel Welch

26. Alan King

27. Michael Parks

28. Millie Perkins

29. Paula Prentiss

30. False (Dennis Price)

31. James Whitmore

32. Paulette Goddard

33. (e)

34) Who sang the title song to the James Bond film, *Octopussy?*

35) Who played the role of Blondie in the film series based upon the comic strip?

36) The role of Dr. Eudora Fletcher in *Zelig* was played by _____.

37) What actor portrayed Tarzan in the 1984 film, *Greystoke?*

38) The role of the boss in *Nine to Five* was performed by what actor?

39) Nelson Eddy and Jeanette MacDonald's final film together was . . .
    a. *I Married an Angel*
    b. *The Chocolate Soldier*
    c. *Knickerbocker Holiday*
    d. *New Moon*
    e. *Sweethearts*

40) What actress played the role of the French schoolteacher opposite Cary Grant in *Father Goose?*

41) What was the name of the chimpanzee that had a feature role in Walt Disney's *Toby Tyler?*

. . . *Answers*

34. Rita Coolidge

35. Penny Singleton

36. Mia Farrow

37. Christopher Lambert

38. Dabney Coleman

39. (a)

40. Leslie Caron

41. Mr. Stubbs

42) Frances Gumm changed names to become . . .
   a. Frances Farmer
   b. Mitzi Gaynor
   c. Cyd Charisse
   d. Barrie Chase
   e. Judy Garland

43) Who won the 1982 Best Actor Oscar?

44) What actor played the role of the sensitive teenage son of Robert Duvall in *The Great Santini?*

45) Meryl Streep won an Academy Award for *Kramer vs. Kramer.* True or False?

46) The film version of *Hair* was directed by . . .
   a. Ken Russell
   b. Herbert Ross
   c. Milos Forman
   d. Ivan Passer
   e. Bob Fosse

47) Actor Troy Donahue had a supporting role in *Godfather II.* True or False?

48) Who portrayed the role of the circus strongwoman in *Adam's Rib?*

49) *Lady L,* starring Sophia Loren and Paul Newman, was written for the screen and directed by _____.

. . . *Answers*

42. (e)

43. Ben Kingsley

44. Michael O'Keefe

45. True

46. (c)

47. True

48. Hope Emerson

49. Peter Ustinov

50) The female lead in the film version of *The Music Man* was played by . . .

    a. Barbara Eden
    b. Shirley Jones
    c. Judy Holliday
    d. Judy Garland
    e. Janet Leigh

51) Who won the Academy Award for cinematography for his work on *Butch Cassidy and the Sundance Kid?*

52) What famous costume designer won an Oscar for her costumes in *The Sting?*

53) What British actor played the role of R2-D2 in *Star Wars?*

54) Who played the role of Lou Canova in Woody Allen's *Broadway Danny Rose?*

55) The film of *Seven Brides for Seven Brothers* was directed by . . .

    a. Gene Kelly
    b. Stanley Donen
    c. Busby Berkeley
    d. Anthony Newley
    e. George Abbott

56) What comic actor played the role of the prizefighter in *Let's Do It Again?*

. . . *Answers*

50. (b)

51. Conrad Hall

52. Edith Head

53. Kenny Baker

54. Nick Apollo Forte

55. (b)

56. Jimmie Walker

QUESTIONS

57) Both *Fritz the Cat* and *Lord of the Rings* were made into animated films by _____.

58) Captain Von Trapp was portrayed in the film version of *The Sound of Music* by . . .
   a. Christopher Plummer
   b. Richard Burton
   c. Dick Van Dyke
   d. Richard Haydn
   e. Max Von Sydow

59) Who played the title role in the 1964 film comedy, *Good Neighbor Sam?*

60) Who played Debra Winger's husband in *Terms of Endearment?*

61) Who played the role of Felix Leiter in *Dr. No?*

62) What was the name of the author who wrote the story upon which the musical film, *Gigi,* was based?

63) Who played the female lead in the film of *Journey to the Center of the Earth?*

64) *Eating Raoul* was written and directed by its star, _____.

65) Who starred in *Easy Money?*

. . . *Answers*

57. Ralph Bakshi

58. (a)

59. Jack Lemmon

60. Jeff Daniels

61. Jack Lord

62. Colette

63. Arlene Dahl

64. Paul Bartel

65. Rodney Dangerfield

66) What actor portrayed the title role in the 1959 film of the musical, *Li'l Abner?*

67) Actress Kay Kendall had a starring role in *The Reluctant Debutante*. True or False?

68) Burt Reynolds, Madeline Kahn and Cybill Shepherd starred in . . .
    a. *Nickelodeon*
    b. *Lovers and Other Strangers*
    c. *At Long Last Love*
    d. *Love With the Proper Stranger*
    e. *The Best Little Whorehouse in Texas*

69) What American actor played the role of the photographer in *Under Fire?*

70) Which of the following films had a prequel?
    a. *The French Connection*
    b. *Butch Cassidy and the Sundance Kid*
    c. *Funny Girl*
    d. *Jaws*
    e. *The Godfather*

71) What actress played twins in Walt Disney's *The Parent Trap?*

72) Woody Allen directed the film version of his play, *Play it Again, Sam*. True or False?

. . . Answers

66. Peter Palmer

67. True

68. (c)

69. Nick Nolte

70. (b)

71. Hayley Mills

72. False (Herbert Ross)

73) Which of the following films did not have a sequel?
   a. *The Godfather*
   b. *The Exorcist*
   c. *The Sting*
   d. *Earthquake*
   e. *The Poseidon Adventure*

74) What actor played the role of the mayor in *Jaws?*

75) What composer-musician-singer turned dramatic actor in the films, *Merry Christmas, Mr. Lawrence, The Hunger* and *Just a Gigolo?*

76) Who began his career as a child star and went on to direct *Eat My Dust, Splash* and *Nightshift?*

77) What Harvard graduate and novelist wrote and directed *Coma, Westworld, The Great Train Robbery* and *Looker?*

78) What writer-director of television's Golden Age directed the comedies, *The One and Only, Where's Poppa?, The Jerk* and *Dead Men Don't Wear Plaid?*

79) Which actor-comedian starred in *The Comic?*
   a. Jack Klugman
   b. Alan Arkin
   c. Dick Van Dyke
   d. Bob Newhart
   e. Henry Winkler

. . . *Answers* .

73. (d)

74. Murray Hamilton

75. David Bowie

76. Ron Howard

77. Michael Crichton

78. Carl Reiner

79. (c)

80) Who directed *Staying Alive?*

81) *Trading Places* starred John Belushi. True or False?

82) Tony Curtis, Jack Lemmon and Natalie Wood starred together in . . .
    a. *Some Like It Hot*
    b. *The Great Race*
    c. *The Pink Panther*
    d. *Penelope*
    e. *The Odd Couple*

83) Who starred in the 1961 film, *The Mongols?*

84) An entire town quit smoking in . . .
    a. *The Russians Are Coming, The Russians Are Coming*
    b. *What a Way to Go*
    c. *Cold Turkey*
    d. *Divorce, American Style*
    e. *The Last Married Couple in America*

85) Who played the female lead opposite Jack Nicholson in Antonioni's *The Passenger?*

86) Who played the role of Dr. Thorndyke in *High Anxiety?*

. . . Answers

80. Sylvester Stallone

81. False (Dan Aykroyd and Eddie Murphy)

82. (b)

83. Jack Palance and Anita Ekberg

84. (c)

85. Maria Schneider

86. Mel Brooks

87) The female lead in *Meet Me in Las Vegas* was played by . . .
   a. Cyd Charisse
   b. Esther Williams
   c. Ginger Rogers
   d. Debbie Reynolds
   e. Ann-Margret

88) *One From the Heart* was directed by _____.

89) *Where the Boys Are* (1960) was directed by _____.

90) Rex Harrison played the unusual title character who maintained a menagerie of furry friends. He played . . .
   a. Dr. Zhivago
   b. Dr. Sardonicus
   c. Dr. Strangelove
   d. Dr. Love
   e. Dr. Doolittle

91) Who played the male lead in *The Last Wave?*

92) Julie Andrews, Carol Channing and Mary Tyler Moore starred together in . . .
   a. *Gentlemen Prefer Blondes*
   b. *Mary Poppins*
   c. *Thoroughly Modern Millie*
   d. *Victor/Victoria*
   e. *Star!*

. . . *Answers*

87. (a)

88. Francis Ford Coppola

89. Henry Levin

90. (e)

91. Richard Chamberlain

92. (c)

93) Who portrayed Sidney Poitier's fiancée in *Guess Who's Coming to Dinner?*

94) What American actor starred in the 1967 film, *Madigan's Millions?*

95) These two comedians flew an airplane through a billboard in *It's A Mad Mad Mad Mad World*. They were . . .
   a. Sid Caesar and Mel Brooks
   b. Dan Rowan and Dick Martin
   c. Stan Laurel and Oliver Hardy
   d. Richard Pryor and Gene Wilder
   e. Buddy Hackett and Mickey Rooney

96) What actor supplied the voice of Darth Vader for the *Star Wars* trilogy?

97) What was the name of the robot in *Forbidden Planet?*

98) Who played Frank Sinatra's younger brother in the film version of *Come Blow Your Horn?*

99) Who played Dirty Harry's sidekick in *The Enforcer?*

100) Who directed the film version of Ray Bradbury's science-fiction fantasy, *Fahrenheit 451?*

101) The Oscar-winning original musical score of Errol Flynn's *The Adventures of Robin Hood* was composed by _____.

. . . *Answers*

93. Katherine Houghton

94. Dustin Hoffman

95. (e)

96. James Earl Jones

97. Robby

98. Tony Bill

99. Tyne Daly

100. Francois Truffaut

101. Erich Wolfgang Korngold

102) *The Treasure of the Sierra Madre* was based upon a novel by _____.

103) Who played the female lead in the western adventure, *The Professionals?*

104) Who played Emilio Zapata's older brother in *Viva Zapata!?*

105) In the original film version of Dickens's *Oliver Twist*, who played Fagin?

106) Cochise, the Apache warrior of *Broken Arrow*, was really what actor?

107) The screenplay of *The Night of the Hunter* was the last film work of _____.

108) *Born Yesterday* starred Judy Holliday and was based upon whose play?

109) The motion picture *Murder, My Sweet,* was based on a novel by _____.

110) *Nanook of the North* was the work of what great documentary filmmaker?

111) Who was the actress turned movie director of *Olympiad?*

... *Answers*

102. B. Traven

103. Claudia Cardinale

104. Anthony Quinn

105. Alec Guiness

106. Jeff Chandler

107. James Agee

108. Garson Kanin

109. Raymond Chandler

110. Robert Flaherty

111. Leni Riefenstahl

112) Who wrote the screenplay to Hitchcock's *Spellbound?*

113) The evil Nazi commander in *Stalag 17* was actually director _____.

114) In *The Great Ziegfield* who portrayed comedienne Fanny Brice?

115) The famed oriental star of *Hell in the Pacific* was _____.

116) The film version of Joshua Logan's *Mister Roberts* has the distinction of having had two directors. They were Mervyn LeRoy and _____.

117) Who played the adolescent son of Lauren Bacall in *The Shootist?*

118) Henry Miller, the author of *Tropic of Cancer,* was portrayed in the film version by _____.

119) Who was the male lead in Barbra Streisand's *Up the Sandbox?*

120) Who directed the commercially successful *The Way We Were?*

121) Who was Bette Davis's female co-star in *Hush . . . Hush, Sweet Charlotte?*

. . . Answers

112. Ben Hecht

113. Otto Preminger

114. herself

115. Toshiro Mifune

116. John Ford

117. Ron Howard

118. Rip Torn

119. David Selby

120. Sydney Pollack

121. Olivia de Havilland

QUESTIONS

122) What British actor played the tour guide in *If It's Tuesday, This Must be Belgium?*

123) *Minnie and Moskowitz* was the work of writer-director _____.

124) Norman Mailer's novel, *The Naked and the Dead,* was filmed by what director?

125) Brian DePalma's *Sisters* cast what actress in the female lead?

126) The adventure film, *Juggernaut,* took place on a _____.

127) In Billy Wilder's comedy, *One, Two, Three,* James Cagney's daughter was played by sex kitten _____.

128) Who portrayed the villain in *Shane?*

129) Who was the male lead in the film version of Jacqueline Susann's *Once is Not Enough?*

130) Who portrayed Bette Midler's chauffeur in *The Rose?*

131) What was the name of Groucho Marx's character in *A Day at the Races?*

132) Who directed *The Magnificent Seven?*

. . . Answers

122. Ian McShane

123. John Cassavetes

124. Raoul Walsh

125. Margot Kidder

126. luxury liner

127. Pamela Tiffin

128. Jack Palance

129. Kirk Douglas

130. Frederic Forrest

131. Hugo Z. Hackenbush

132. John Sturges

133) *Raiders of the Lost Ark* had a screenplay by _____.

134) In the 1969 version of *Hamlet,* who played the title role?

135) The two lead actresses in *The Haunting* were Julie Harris and _____.

136) Who played Philip Marlowe in *The Long Goodbye* (1973)?

137) Peter Sellers's comedy, *The Party,* was written and directed by _____.

138) Who portrayed the lead in *The Story of Adele H?*

139) Roger Corman's *The Cry Baby Killer* marked the film debut of what actor?

140) *There Was a Crooked Man . . .* is the work of what film director?

141) Who was the male lead in Walter Hill's *The Driver?*

142) Who composed the original musical score to *The Fall of the Roman Empire?*

143) Who produced *55 Days at Peking?*

. . . Answers

133. Lawrence Kasdan

134. Nicol Williamson

135. Claire Bloom

136. Elliott Gould

137. Blake Edwards

138. Isabelle Adjani

139. Jack Nicholson

140. Joseph L. Mankiewicz

141. Ryan O'Neal

142. Dimitri Tiomkin

143. Samuel Bronston

144) *In the Heat of the Night* had cinematography by
_____.

145) In *The Great Escape,* who played the character of the "Scrounger"?

146) In *Robin and Marian,* the Sheriff of Nottingham was portrayed by what well-known actor?

147) Marsha Mason's ten-year-old daughter in *The Goodbye Girl* was played by what actress?

148) *Million Dollar Legs* was a comedy vehicle for what comic?

149) Who directed the original version of *The Postman Always Rings Twice?*

150) Who wrote the script for the film, *The Gambler?*

151) Who played Paul Newman's daughter in *The Life and Times of Judge Roy Bean?*

152) Who wrote the zither music found in *The Third Man?*

153) Who portrayed the hero of the film version of John Barth's *The End of the Road?*

154) Who directed the film version of *Equus?*

. . . *Answers*

144. Haskell Wexler

145. James Garner

146. Robert Shaw

147. Quinn Cummings

148. W.C. Fields

149. Tay Garnett

150. James Toback

151. Jacqueline Bisset

152. Anton Karas

153. Stacy Keach

154. Sidney Lumet

155) Who played the detective in *The Exorcist?*

156) Robert Aldrich's *Hustle* took place in what city?

157) Who composed the music for Steven Spielberg's *E. T. The Extra-terrestrial?*

158) What won the Oscar for Best Picture in 1982?

159) *Slither* was the first film directed by _____.

160) Who played the character of Posey in *The Dirty Dozen?*

161) Jack Lemmon's henchman in *The Great Race* was played by what actor?

162) Who directed *Papillon?*

163) Who wrote the screenplay for *Spartacus?*

164) *Risky Business* was written and directed by _____.

165) What actor died during the filming of *Twilight Zone: The Movie?*

166) Who wrote the Oscar-winning musical score for *Lawrence of Arabia?*

. . . *Answers*

155. Lee J. Cobb

156. Los Angeles

157. John Williams

158. *Gandhi*

159. Howard Zieff

160. Clint Walker

161. Peter Falk

162. Franklin Schaffner

163. Dalton Trumbo

164. Paul Brickman

165. Vic Morrow

166. Maurice Jarre

QUESTIONS

167) Who played the title role in Richard Brooks's film version of Joseph Conrad's *Lord Jim?*

168) *The Private Navy of Sgt. O'Farrell* was a film vehicle for what comedy star?

169) Thomas Hardy's *Far from the Madding Crowd* was brought to the screen by what director?

170) *2001: A Space Odyssey* was originally shown in a process known as _____.

171) *Half a Sixpence* starred what British music hall entertainer?

172) *Star!* was the screen biography of what actress?

173) Who directed *Hurry Sundown?*

174) Dustin Hoffman's father in *The Graduate* was portrayed by whom?

175) Who directed the auto racing spectacular, *Grand Prix?*

176) The setting for the film, *Sand Pebbles,* was the country of _____.

177) *Play Misty for Me* marked whose directorial debut?

. . . *Answers*

167. Peter O'Toole

168. Bob Hope

169. John Schlesinger

170. Cinerama

171. Tommy Steele

172. Gertrude Lawrence

173. Otto Preminger

174. William Daniels

175. John Frankenheimer

176. China

177. Clint Eastwood

178) *The Only Game in Town* teamed superstars Elizabeth Taylor and _____.

179) *Ocean's Eleven* involved a robbery in what city?

180) Who played the female lead in Stanley Donen's *Arabesque?*

181) Who composed the music for the John Wayne film, *Hatari?*

182) Sean Connery and _____ starred as the male leads in *The Molly Maguires.*

183) Who directed *The Man Who Would Be King?*

184) Who directed *Little Big Man?*

185) Who won the Best Supporting Actor Oscar for his performance in *Cool Hand Luke?*

186) In *The Sting,* who played the character of Henry Gondorff?

187) *Oh! What a Lovely War* marked whose directorial debut?

188) In *Khartoum,* Charlton Heston played the part of _____.

. . . *Answers*

178. Warren Beatty

179. Las Vegas

180. Sophia Loren

181. Henry Mancini

182. Richard Harris

183. John Huston

184. Arthur Penn

185. George Kennedy

186. Paul Newman

187. Richard Attenborough

188. Charles "Chinese" Gordon

189) Who directed the film version of the musical *Camelot?*

190) *The Wiz* was set in what city?

191) Who directed the film version of *The Odd Couple?*

192) What actor played the lead role of a skier in *Downhill Racer?*

193) Who directed both *The Three Musketeers* ad *The Four Musketeers?*

194) The theme song to the James Bond adventure, *Live and Let Die,* was composed and performed by _____.

195) Who starred in *Le Mans?*

196) Who directed Philip Roth's *Goodbye, Columbus?*

197) Who composed the music for the 1963 version of *Cleopatra?*

198) *The King of Marvin Gardens* starred Jack Nicholson and was directed by _____.

199) In the film version of *Auntie Mame,* who played Agnes Gooch?

200) Who directed *Finian's Rainbow?*

. . . *Answers*

189. Joshua Logan

190. New York

191. Gene Saks

192. Robert Redford

193. Richard Lester

194. Paul McCartney

195. Steve McQueen

196. Larry Peerce

197. Alex North

198. Bob Rafelson

199. Peggy Cass

200. Francis Coppola

201) *The Incredible Shrinking Woman* starred _____ in the title role.

202) Who played the female lead in the 1976 version of *King Kong?*

203) In *The President's Analyst,* who played the psychoanalyst.

204) Alain Resnais's *Stavisky* had a musical score composed by _____.

205) In the 1948 version of *The Three Musketeers,* who portrayed the role of Lady de Winter?

206) The science fiction film, *THX-1138,* marked whose directorial debut?

207) Actress Carole Lombard died in a plane crash following her completion of her role in _____.

208) In *To Kill a Mockingbird,* who portrayed the role of Boo Radley?

209) Who played the title role in the historical film, *Cromwell?*

210) Who directed *The Day of the Dolphin?*

211) Who played the role of Napoleon in *Desiree?*

. . . Answers

201. Lily Tomlin

202. Jessica Lange

203. James Coburn

204. Stephen Sondheim

205. Lana Turner

206. George Lucas

207. *To Be or Not to Be*

208. Robert Duvall

209. Richard Harris

210. Mike Nichols

211. Marlon Brando

212) Who wrote the screenplay of *Dr. Zhivago?*

213) Who directed the film, *$?*

214) In *The Eyes of Laura Mars,* who played the role of photographer Laura Mars?

215) Who played the bride in *Father of the Bride?*

216) Who directed *The Hindenburg?*

217) In *John and Mary,* the role of John was played by Dustin Hoffman. Who played Mary?

218) Who wrote the screenplay for *Network?*

219) In the 1939 version of *Stagecoach,* who played the role of the Ringo Kid?

220) Who directed *The Stunt Man?*

221) *The Sugarland Express* marked whose directorial debut?

222) In the film, *True Confessions,* the two brothers were played by Robert Duvall and _____.

223) *The 300 Spartans* starred what actor?

224) The first Academy Award for Best Picture was awarded to the 1927 production _____.

. . . *Answers*

212. Robert Bolt

213. Richard Brooks

214. Faye Dunaway

215. Elizabeth Taylor

216. Robert Wise

217. Mia Farrow

218. Paddy Chayevsky

219. John Wayne

220. Richard Rush

221. Steven Spielberg

222. Robert DeNiro

223. Richard Egan

224. *Wings*

225) George Segal played Dick and _____ played Jane in *Fun with Dick and Jane*.

226) The comedy *Knock on Wood*, was a vehicle for what comedian?

227) Who directed the film, *Loving?*

228) The character of Brigid O'Shaughnessy in *The Maltese Falcon* was played by what actress?

229) Who directed the film of Robert Bolt's play, *A Man for All Seasons?*

230) In *Man on a Swing*, the role of the clairvoyant was played by what actor?

231) Who played the part of Melvin Dummar in *Melvin and Howard?*

232) The western, *One-Eyed Jacks*, starred and was directed by what actor?

233) John Frankenheimer's *Seconds*, starred _____ as the "reborn" banker.

234) Who directed the documentary epic, *The Sorrow and the Pity?*

235) In *Taxi Driver*, who played the role of the adolescent prostitute?

. . . Answers

225. Jane Fonda

226. Danny Kaye

227. Irvin Kershner

228. Mary Astor

229. Fred Zinneman

230. Joel Grey

231. Paul Le Mat

232. Marlon Brando

233. Rock Hudson

234. Marcel Ophuls

235. Jodie Foster

236) Who directed the comedy, *The Guide for the Married Man?*

237) Who portrayed the title role in *Gigot?*

238) *Nevada Smith* was a spin-off from the film of the novel entitled _____.

239) Who directed *For a Few Dollars More?*

240) Who played the female lead in *The Next Man?*

241) Who directed the 1981 film, *Pennies from Heaven?*

242) In *Saratoga Trunk,* who played adventuress Clio Duaine?

243) The Academy Award-winning screenplay for *In the Heat of the Night* was written by _____.

244) What French actor starred in the highly successful foreign thriller, *That Man from Rio?*

245) *The Ipcress File* starred what British actor as a spy?

246) *L'Avventura* was directed by what Italian filmmaker?

247) The science-fiction sex fantasy, *Barbarella,* was a starring vehicle for what actress?

. . . Answers

236. Gene Kelly

237. Jackie Gleason

238. *The Carpetbaggers*

239. Sergio Leone

240. Cornelia Sharpe

241. Herbert Ross

242. Ingrid Bergman

243. Stirling Silliphant

244. Jean-Paul Belmondo

245. Michael Caine

246. Michelangelo Antonioni

247. Jane Fonda

248) Herman Melville's short novel, *Billy Budd,* was directed as a film by what actor-writer?

249) *Body Heat* took place in what state?

250) *Bound for Glory* depicted the life of singer-composer Woody Guthrie. Who portrayed him?

251) Who played Julius Caesar in the 1946 version of *Caesar and Cleopatra?*

252) In *Cast a Giant Shadow,* Colonel "Mickey" Marcus was portrayed by what actor?

253) *Gigi* was directed by what Oscar-winning director?

254) Who played the crazy, drunk gunslinger in *Cat Ballou?*

255) In Mike Nichols's version of *Catch-22,* the central role of Yossarian was portrayed by what actor?

256) Academy Award-winning actress _____ won an Oscar for her supporting role in the film version of *West Side Story.*

257) Who portrayed runner Harold Abrahams in the highly acclaimed *Chariots of Fire?*

258) The comedy-drama, *Georgy Girl,* starred what actress?

. . . Answers

248. Peter Ustinov

249. Florida

250. David Carradine

251. Claude Rains

252. Kirk Douglas

253. Vincente Minnelli

254. Lee Marvin

255. Alan Arkin

256. Rita Moreno

257. Ben Cross

258. Lynn Redgrave

259) Who played the lead role in *Charley Varrick?*

260) *Chloe in the Afternoon* was written and directed by _____.

261) Who played *Hercules* in the 1957 version?

262) The alleged rape victim in *Anatomy of a Murder* was portrayed by actress _____.

263) Who won an Oscar for Best Director for *Tom Jones?*

264) Who played the lead role in *Charly?*

265) Who played the part of Miss Place in *Butch Cassidy and the Sundance Kid.*

266) Who directed the highly acclaimed film version of *Women in Love?*

267) The lead role in *The Reincarnation of Peter Proud* was played by _____.

268) What conductor created the musical score for *Fantasia?*

269) Who composed the music for the popular title song to *Three Coins in the Fountain?*

270) The male lead in Otto Preminger's *The Cardinal* was portrayed by what actor?

. . . *Answers*

259. Walter Matthau

260. Eric Rohmer

261. Steve Reeves

262. Lee Remick

263. Tony Richardson

264. Cliff Robertson

265. Katherine Ross

266. Ken Russell

267. Michael Sarrazin

268. Leopold Stokowski

269. Jule Styne

270. Tom Tryon

271) Who directed the film version of *Fame?*

272) In *The Lady Eve,* the male lead was a millionaire scientist played by what actor?

273) The 1971 film adaptation of Shakespeare's *Macbeth* was directed by _____.

274) Who portrayed the Queen of Sheba in *Solomon and Sheba?*

275) The landmark "skin flick," *The Immoral Mr. Teas,* was directed by _____.

276) Mickey Mouse was briefly known as _____.

277) Who portrayed the female lead in *The Counterfeit Traitor?*

278) The 1977 French film *The Man Who Loved Women* was directed by _____.

279) Who played the role of the nurse-housekeeper in Hitchcock's *Rear Window?*

280) In Billy Wilder's 1970 film, *The Private Life of Sherlock Holmes,* the role of Inspector Holmes was portrayed by what actor?

281) Who was the male lead in Orson Welles's film of Kafka's *The Trial?*

. . . *Answers*

271. Alan Parker

272. Henry Fonda

273. Roman Polanski

274. Gina Lollobrigida

275. Russ Meyer

276. Mortimer Mouse

277. Lili Palmer

278. Francois Truffaut

279. Thelma Ritter

280. Robert Stephens

281. Anthony Perkins

282) Who produced *Heat?*

283) Who played the title role in *Prince Valiant?*

284) In the 1953 version of *The Jazz Singer,* who portrayed the leading role?

285) Sidney Poitier's Oscar-winning role in *Lilies of the Field* was directed by _____.

286) Who was the female lead in *Still of the Night?*

287) *Heller in Pink Tights* was the only western directed by _____.

288) The Academy Award-winning screenplay for *The Sting* was written by _____.

289) Who directed the film *Shaft?*

290) The film version of *The Time Machine* was based upon a novel by whom?

291) Hitchcock's *Torn Curtain* starred Julie Andrews and actor _____.

292) Who directed both *David and Lisa* and *Mommie Dearest?*

293) Actor Tyrone Power died of a heart attack while filming what movie?

. . . *Answers*

282. Andy Warhol

283. Robert Wagner

284. Danny Thomas

285. Ralph Nelson

286. Meryl Streep

287. George Cukor

288. David S. Ward

289. Gordon Parks

290. H.G. Wells

291. Paul Newman

292. Frank Perry

293. *Solomon and Sheba*

294) The Monkees' film, *Head,* was written by Bob Rafelson and what actor?

295) *The Towering Inferno* was produced by two major Hollywood studios. One was Warner Brothers. What was the other?

296) In the film version of *Inherit the Wind,* the character representing Scopes was portrayed by what actor?

297) *Inside Daisy Clover* starred Natalie Wood and Robert Redford. Who was the director?

298) Actor Joe Yule, Jr. changed his name to _____.

299) What playwright wrote the screenplay for *The Last Tycoon?*

300) The lead role in the screen version of *The Other Side of Midnight* was portrayed by what actress?

301) Who directed *Excalibur?*

302) In Stanley Kubrick's *Lolita,* who played the character of Clair Quilty?

303) William Franklin Beedle, Jr. became a popular actor and changed his name to _____.

304) Who won an Oscar for his cinematography on *Hud?*

. . . *Answers*

294. Jack Nicholson

295. 20th Century Fox

296. Dick York

297. Robert Mulligan

298. Mickey Rooney

299. Harold Pinter

300. Marie-France Pisier

301. John Boorman

302. Peter Sellers

303. William Holden

304. James Wong Howe

305) Who portrayed the title role in the film version of *The Elephant Man?*

306) The role of Ma Kettle was played by what actress?

307) Who directed Walt Disney's *Pollyanna?*

308) *Easy Rider*'s star and director was _____.

309) Who sang the theme song to the film *Gunfight at the O.K. Corral?*

310) The film *Billy Jack* was written, directed and acted by _____.

311) Who portrayed the inquisitive Miss Marple in four films based upon Agatha Christie stories?

312) What playwright wrote the original screenplay for *The Chase?*

313) Who composed the musical score for *Citizen Kane?*

314) Who produced and directed *The Defiant Ones?*

315) John Osborn's play, *The Entertainer,* was made into a film in 1960 starring what actor?

316) The science-fiction fantasy, *Fantastic Voyage,* was directed by whom?

. . . *Answers*

305. John Hurt

306. Marjorie Main

307. David Swift

308. Dennis Hopper

309. Frankie Laine

310. Tom Laughlin

311. Dame Margaret Rutherford

312. Lillian Hellman

313. Bernard Herrmann

314. Stanley Kramer

315. Laurence Olivier

316. Richard Fleischer

317) *Goin' South* was directed by what popular actor?

318) The musical score to *The Magnificent Seven* was composed by _____.

319) Who played the role of Ethan Edwards in *The Searchers?*

320) Who directed the thriller *Sorry, Wrong Number?*

321) Who played the female lead in *Summer Wishes, Winter Dreams?*

322) The film, *Time Bandits,* contains songs composed by what musician?

323) *The Bliss of Mrs. Blossom* starred what actress in the title role?

324) *The Black Bird,* a comedy spoof on *The Maltese Falcon,* starred what actor?

325) Who directed *Cinderella Liberty?*

326) The lead character in Fellini's *8½* was portrayed by what actor?

327) *Sullivan's Travels* was written and directed by _____.

. . . Answers

317. Jack Nicholson

318. Elmer Bernstein

319. John Wayne

320. Anatole Litvak

321. Joanne Woodward

322. George Harrison

323. Shirley MacLaine

324. George Segal

325. Mark Rydell

326. Marcello Mastroianni

327. Preston Sturges

QUESTIONS

328) The female lead in *Lady L* was portrayed by what actress?

329) The musical score for *Last Tango in Paris* was composed and performed by _____.

330) King Henry II was portrayed by what actor in the film version of *The Lion in Winter.*

331) Who portrayed the title role in *Fellini's Casanova?*

332) *Gold* took place in what country?

333) In the 1969 musical remake of *Goodbye, Mr. Chips,* who played Mrs. Chips?

334) The role of Cardinal Wolsey in *A Man for all Seasons* was the work of what actor?

335) Who composed the Academy Award-winning music of *Midnight Express?*

336) The male lead in *The Owl and the Pussycat* was played by what actor?

337) Who directed the film, *The Prime of Miss Jean Brodie?*

338) The role of Emma Goldman in *Reds* was portrayed by what actress?

. . . Answers

328. Sophia Loren

329. Gato Barbieri

330. Peter O'Toole

331. Donald Sutherland

332. South Africa

333. Petula Clark

334. Orson Welles

335. Giorgio Moroder

336. George Segal

337. Ronald Neame

338. Maureen Stapleton

339) In *The Bible*, the voice of God was provided by _____.

340) The wise-cracking detective in *The Big Fix* was played by what actor?

341) The thriller, *Blow-Out*, was directed by whom?

342) The leading role in Walt Disney's *Third Man on the Mountain* was portrayed by what actor?

343) *Blue Collar* marked the directorial debut of what screenwriter?

344) Who was the cinematographer of *Citizen Kane?*

345) The young ballerina in Chaplin's *Limelight* was played by what actress?

346) In the film version of the musical, *The Unsinkable Molly Brown*, who was the male lead?

347) The female lead in *T.R. Baskin* was portrayed by _____.

348) Who played the female lead in *Sounder.*

349) What black actor-comedian starred in *Which Way Is Up?*

. . . *Answers*

339. John Huston

340. Richard Dreyfuss

341. Brian DePalma

342. James MacArthur

343. Paul Shrader

344. Gregg Toland

345. Claire Bloom

346. Harve Presnell

347. Candice Bergen

348. Cicely Tyson

349. Richard Pryor

350) What actor played the lead in the remake of *Breathless?*

351) Who wrote the script for *Pretty Poison?*

352) Who directed *Will Penny?*

353) The female lead in *The Great Santini* was portrayed by what actress?

354) *A New Leaf* was written and directed by what comedienne?

355) Who played Clark Gable in *Gable and Lombard?*

356) Who portrayed the title character in *The Bitch?*

357) *Targets,* starring Boris Karloff, marked the directorial debut of whom?

358) Who was the female lead in *Sunday, Bloody Sunday?*

359) *The Garden of the Finzi-Continis* was directed by what Italian filmmaker?

360) The role of Miss Moneypenny in most of the James Bond films has been played by what actress?

361) Who directed the country-and-western musical *Nashville?*

. . . Answers

350. Richard Gere

351. Lorenzo Semple, Jr.

352. Tom Gries

353. Blythe Danner

354. Elaine May

355. James Brolin

356. Joan Collins

357. Peter Bogdanovich

358. Glenda Jackson

359. Vittorio DeSica

360. Lois Maxwell

361. Robert Altman

QUESTIONS

562) The role of Louis XVI, opposite Norma Shearer in *Marie Antoinette,* was played by what actor?

563) The male lead in the film, *Thief,* was portrayed by what actor?

564) What singer had a supporting role in *Journey to the Center of the Earth?*

565) Who played the title role in the 1977 film *Valentino?*

566) Who portrayed the female lead in *Big Bad Mama?*

567) Who directed *Gone With the Wind?*

568) The role of the circus manager in *The Greatest Show on Earth* was played by what actor?

569) The Marx Brothers made their screen debut in the film version of what play?

570) Who played the female lead in *Summer of '42?*

571) Who wrote the script for *It's a Mad Mad Mad Mad World?*

572) What actor made his feature film debut in *The Devil's Rain?*

573) The role of the elderly father in *I Never Sang for My Father* was played by what actor?

. . . Answers

362. Robert Morley

363. James Caan

364. Pat Boone

365. Rudolf Nureyev

366. Angie Dickinson

367. Victor Fleming

368. Charlton Heston

369. *The Cocoanuts*

370. Jennifer O'Neill

371. William Rose

372. John Travolta

373. Melvyn Douglas

374) In *The Godfather,* who played the role of Moe Green?

375) The film, *Conformist,* is based upon a novel by _____.

376) Who directed *No Way to Treat a Lady?*

377) Who played the female lead in *Marathon Man?*

378) Who directed *Our Man Flint?*

379) The role of the sexy skindiver in the James Bond film, *Dr. No,* was played by what actress?

380) The title role in *Zorro, the Gay Blade,* was portrayed by what actor?

381) Who made her screen debut as Bette Davis's daughter in Frank Capra's *Pocketful of Miracles?*

382) In *Scrooge,* the musical version of *A Christmas Carol,* the title role was performed by what actor?

383) Who played the male lead in John Ford's film of *The Hurricane?*

384) Who directed *Anne of the Thousand Days?*

385) Who created the popular cartoon character "Woody Woodpecker"?

. . . *Answers*

374. Alex Rocco

375. Alberto Moravia

376. Jack Smight

377. Marthe Keller

378. Daniel Mann

379. Ursula Andress

380. George Hamilton

381. Ann-Margret

382. Albert Finney

383. Jon Hall

384. Charles Jarrott

385. Walter Lantz

386) Who portrayed the knight in Ingmar Bergman's *Seventh Seal?*

387) Who directed the 1952 version of *The Thing?*

388) The title role in *The Amorous Adventures of Moll Flanders* was played by what actress?

389) Who played Aunt Marsh in the 1933 version of *Little Women?*

390) The script for *Rancho Deluxe* was written by what novelist?

391) Who produced *Ragtime?*

392) Who directed the 1946 film entitled *Gilda?*

393) In the comedy *How to Murder Your Wife,* husband Jack Lemmon is out to kill his wife, portrayed by _____.

394) Who directed the musical *New York, New York?*

395) The largest film set ever built was for the 1964 production of _____.

396) Alexandra Zuck changed her name for Hollywood to _____.

. . . *Answers*

386. Max von Sydow

387. Christian Nyby

388. Kim Novak

389. Edna May Oliver

390. Thomas McGuane

391. Dino De Laurentiis

392. Charles Vidor

393. Virna Lisi

394. Martin Scorsese

395. *The Fall of the Roman Empire*

396. Sandra Dee

397) Who has won the most Best Actress Oscar awards?

398) Who was the second male actor to refuse a Best Actor Oscar?

399) The highest price ever paid for film rights was paid for the rights to _____.

400) In *The Wind and the Lion,* who played President Theodore Roosevelt?

401) Who directed the film of the successful novel, *The Group?*

402) In the film version of *The Grapes of Wrath,* who played the role of Ma Joad?

403) What was the name of the college professor Groucho Marx portrayed in *Horsefeathers?*

404) What French actor played the role of the evil Drax in the James Bond thriller, *Moonraker?*

405) Who directed *Ride the High Country,* starring Joel McCrea and Randolph Scott?

406) In the 1964 film of *Zorba the Greek,* who played the young Englishman?

407) The irreverent film comedy, *Putney Swope,* was written and directed by _____.

. . . Answers

397. Katherine Hepburn

398. Marlon Brando

399. *Annie*

400. Brian Keith

401. Sidney Lumet

402. Jane Darwell

403. Quincy Adams Wagstaff

404. Michel Lonsdale

405. Sam Peckinpah

406. Alan Bates

407. Robert Downey

408) What actress had the role of the kidnap victim in *The Collector?*

409) What actress made her screen debut in Hitchcock's *The Trouble With Harry?*

410) What British film director was responsible for making *O Lucky Man!?*

411) In Cecil B. De Mille's *The Ten Commandments,* the role of Nefertiti was played by what actress?

412) The hero in the film, *The Oscar,* was portrayed by what actor?

413) What well-known screenwriter was responsible for writing and directing *Personal Best?*

414) Who was the female lead in *Saturday Night Fever?*

415) In Ken Russell's *The Music Lovers,* the central role of Tchaikovsky was performed by what actor?

416) Who was the male lead in *Gidget?*

417) Who played Benjamin Franklin in the film version of *1776?*

418) In the science-fiction film, *Zardoz,* the lead role was played by what actor?

419) Who played Pretty Boy Floyd in *Young Dillinger?*

. . . *Answers*

408. Samantha Eggar

409. Shirley MacLaine

410. Lindsay Anderson

411. Anne Baxter

412. Stephen Boyd

413. Robert Towne

414. Karen Lynn Gorney

415. Richard Chamberlain

416. James Darren

417. Howard da Silva

418. Sean Connery

419. Robert Conrad

420) Who was the writer-director-producer of *Enter Laughing?*

421) Who wrote *Pillow Talk?*

422) Who directed the 1942 version of *Cat People?*

423) Who acted the role of Richard the Lionhearted in the film of *The Lion in Winter?*

424) The Academy Award-winning score for *Lili* was composed by _____.

425) Who played sleuth Hercule Poirot in *Murder on the Orient Express?*

426) Who wrote the screenplay for the film, *Judgment at Nuremberg?*

427) What actor recreated his stage role in the film version of *Equus?*

428) Who directed the film of the musical *Porgy and Bess?*

429) Who produced *Nicholas and Alexandra?*

430) Who played the role of Cornelius's mate in *Planet of the Apes?*

431) What actor played Woody Allen's best friend in *Annie Hall?*

. . . Answers

420. Carl Reiner

421. Stanley Shapiro

422. Jacques Tourneur

423. Anthony Hopkins

424. Bronislaw Kaper

425. Albert Finney

426. Abby Mann

427. Peter Firth

428. Otto Preminger

429. Sam Spiegel

430. Kim Hunter

431. Tony Roberts

432) Who directed *Champion?*

433) The 1927 epic *Napoleon* was directed by what French filmmaker?

434) Who wrote the screenplay to *Just Tell Me What You Want?*

435) Who played the title character in *Lady Caroline Lamb?*

436) The lavish musical, *Thoroughly Modern Millie,* was produced by whom?

437) Who had the male lead in *Pretty Baby?*

438) What actor starred in the film version of *Flower Drum Song?*

439) Who won the Best Actress Oscar for *Norma Rae?*

440) In the 1954 film of the Broadway hit, *Top Banana,* who recreated his lead role.

441) In both *Godfather* films, who played the role of Mrs. Michael Corleone.

442) *The Late Show* was written and directed by whom?

. . . *Answers*

432. Mark Robson

433. Abel Gance

434. Jay Presson Allen

435. Sarah Miles

436. Ross Hunter

437. Keith Carradine

438. James Shigeta

439. Sally Field

440. Phil Silvers

441. Diane Keaton

442. Robert Benton

QUESTIONS

443) The role of Sarah Brown in the film version of *Guys and Dolls* was portrayed by what actress?

444) The hit comedy film, *Trading Places,* was directed by whom?

445) Who played the female lead in the film of *Stop the World—I Want to Get Off?*

446) Who played the female lead in *The Paper Chase?*

447) Who directed *The Story of Louis Pasteur?*

448) Who portrayed multiple roles in *The Seven Faces of Dr. Lao?*

449) Who played the sensual female lead in *The Night Porter?*

450) Who wrote the music for the musical version of *Lost Horizon?*

451) Who played the male lead opposite Doris Day in the 1963 comedy, *The Thrill of It All?*

452) Who directed the 1931 version of *Frankenstein?*

453) Who wrote the songs for the musical film of *Popeye?*

454) What American city was the background for the 1983 comedy hit, *Risky Business?*

. . . *Answers*

443. Jean Simmons

444. John Landis

445. Millicent Martin

446. Lindsay Wagner

447. Irving Rapper

448. Tony Randall

449. Charlotte Rampling

450. Burt Bacharach

451. James Garner

452. James Whale

453. Harry Nilsson

454. Chicago

455) Who played the title role in the film farce, *Dr. Detroit?*

456) In the original film version of *M*A*S*H*, what actress portrayed "Hot Lips" Houlihan?

457) The role of the Snake in the 1974 musical version of *The Little Prince* was played by whom?

458) Who played the role of Nancy Ashford in the 1954 film, *Magnificent Obsession?*

459) What is the title of French director Jacques Demy's first American film, made in 1969?

460) Who portrayed Lady Macbeth in Orson Welles's *Macbeth.*

461) What well-known author received co-screenwriting credit with director John Huston for the adaptation of *Moby Dick?*

462) What actress won the Best Supporting Actress Oscar for *Network?*

463) Who directed *Ordinary People?*

464) *A Place in the Sun* is based upon a novel by Edna Ferber. True or False?

465) Who directed *Silver Streak?*

. . . *Answers*

455. Dan Aykroyd

456. Sally Kellerman

457. Bob Fosse

458. Agnes Moorehead

459. *The Model Shop*

460. Jeanette Nolan

461. Ray Bradbury

462. Beatrice Straight

463. Robert Redford

464. False (Theodore Dreiser)

465. Arthur Hiller

466) Who directed the 1970 film, *The Grasshopper*, which starred Jacqueline Bisset?

467) German director Rainer Werner Fassbinder directed *The Mystery of Kaspar Hauser*. True or False?

468) Who directed Laurence Olivier's performance in the lead role of *Richard III?*

469) Al Jolson was played by Larry Blyden in *The Jolson Story*. True or False?

470) Who played the male lead opposite Audrey Hepburn in *Breakfast at Tiffany's?*

471) Who played Superman's mother in *Superman?*

472) The music for the film, *Superfly*, was composed by Earth, Wind & Fire. True or False?

473) Who portrayed George Raft in *The George Raft Story?*

474) Who had the role of the tough cop in *McQ?*

475) The Oscar-winning screenplay for *Darling* was written by Joe Orton. True or False?

476) What classic play was the source for Joseph L. Mankiewicz's *The Honey Pot?*

. . . Answers

466. Jerry Paris

467. False (Werner Herzog)

468. himself

469. False (Larry Parks)

470. George Peppard

471. Susannah York

472. False (Curtis Mayfield)

473. Ray Danton

474. John Wayne

475. False (Frederic Raphael)

476. *Volpone*

QUESTIONS

477) *The Fixer* took place in what European country?

478) Who directed the 1967 prison film *Cool Hand Luke?*

479) Who was the director of photography for *Carnal Knowledge?*

480) *The Friends of Eddie Coyle* was directed by Peter Yates. True or False?

481) Who played Desdemona in the 1965 film of *Othello?*

482) Who played the title role of *Genghis Khan* in the 1965 film?

483) Who directed *Wild in the Streets?*

484) *True Grit* was the sequel to *Rooster Cogburn*. True or False?

485) What actor starred opposite Marlon Brandon in *Apocalypse Now?*

486) Who had the female lead in *Diary of a Mad House-wife?*

487) The 1954 version of *Romeo and Juliet* was directed by Franco Zeffirelli. True or False?

... Answers

477. Russia

478. Stuart Rosenberg

479. Giuseppe Rotunno

480. True

481. Maggie Smith

482. Omar Sharif

483. Barry Shear

484. False (*Rooster Cogburn* was the sequel)

485. Martin Sheen

486. Carrie Snodgrass

487. False (Renato Castellani)

488) Who portrayed the title character in *The Wicked Dreams of Paula Schultz?*

489) What American city was the background for *Three Days of the Condor?*

490) Who played the role of Jaws in *Moonraker?*

491) The comedy, *So Fine,* was written and directed by whom?

492) Who played the role of Crassus in Stanley Kubrick's *Spartacus?*

493) Who directed the 1968 western, *Five Card Stud?*

494) Who portrayed the eccentric lady passenger and won an Oscar for it in *Airport?*

495) What actor played the lead in the film version of *A Bell for Adano?*

496) What well-known sexpot had a role in *Will Success Spoil Rock Hunter?*

497) Who played Richard III in the 1939 film, *Tower Of London?*

498) What playwright wrote the story and screenplay for *The Yellow Rolls Royce?*

. . . Answers

488. Elke Sommer

489. New York City

490. Richard Kiel

491. Andrew Bergman

492. Laurence Olivier

493. Henry Hathaway

494. Helen Hayes

495. John Hodiak

496. Jayne Mansfield

497. Basil Rathbone

498. Sir Terrence Rattigan

499) Who directed the 1977 Sophia Loren-Marcello Mastroianni film, *A Special Day?*

500) *Hud* was written by Irving Ravetch and _____ .

501) Who produced the musical extravaganza, *Dr. Doolittle?*

502) Who won the Academy Award for Best Supporting Actor for his role in *The Big Country?*

503) What actress portrayed Honey Bruce in Bob Fosse's *Lenny?*

504) Who portrayed Jim, the runaway slave, in the 1939 film version of *The Adventures of Huckleberry Finn?*

505) Who was the writer-director of the thriller, *Capricorn One?*

506) Who was the female lead in *American Gigolo?*

507) *The Legend of Lylah Clare* was directed by George Cukor. True or False?

508) Who directed *Little Fauss and Big Halsy?*

509) Who directed *I Shot Jesse James?*

510) Who portrayed Gene Hackman's French sidekick in *French Connection II?*

. . . Answers

499. Ettore Scola

500. Harriet Frank, Jr.

501. Arthur P. Jacobs

502. Burl Ives

503. Valerie Perrine

504. Rex Ingram

505. Peter Hyams

506. Lauren Hutton

507. False (Robert Aldrich)

508. Sidney J. Furie

509. Sam Fuller

510. Bernard Fresson

511) What actor played the title role in *Youngblood Hawke?*

512) Who directed the 1973 film, *A Touch of Class?*

513) What singer had a leading role as one of the girls in the 1960 version of *Whree The Boys Are?*

514) What male actor played the romantic lead in the 1979 film, *Hanover Street?*

515) What actor directed his first film in 1971, entitled *The Hired Hand?*

516) Who directed *Rolling Thunder?*

517) What actress won a Best Actress Oscar for *One Flew Over the Cuckoo's Nest?*

518) Who played Father Fitzgibbon in *Going My Way?*

519) The heiress in *The Fortune* was portrayed by what actress?

520) Who composed the haunting film score for *The Exorcist?*

521) What American actor had the male lead in the 1980 film, *The Competition?*

522) Who played David Niven's sidekick in *Around the World in 80 Days?*

... Answers

511. James Franciscus

512. Melvin Frank

513. Connie Stevens

514. Harrison Ford

515. Peter Fonda

516. John Flynn

517. Louise Fletcher

518. Barry Fitzgerald

519. Stockard Channing

520. Mike Oldfield

521. Richard Dreyfuss

522. Cantinflas

523) Who played Igor in Mel Brooks's *Young Franken-stein?*

524) What well-known actor received an Oscar nomination for his work in *Murder Inc.?*

525) Who played the role of Peter in the 1978 film, *Jesus of Nazareth?*

526) Who played the young male supporting role in *North to Alaska?*

527) Producer Robert Evans had a brief career as an actor. True or False?

528) What famous British actress was acclaimed for her performance in *The Whisperers?*

529) Who wrote the 1964 film, *Send Me No Flowers?*

530) Who directed the award winning short film, *Occurrence at Owl Creek Bridge?*

531) Who directed the 1971 rock western, *Zachariah?*

532) Who played the attorney in *Compulsion?*

533) What world famous actress starred in Fellini's *La Dolce Vita?*

. . . Answers

523. Marty Feldman

524. Peter Falk

525. James Farentino

526. Fabian

527. True

528. Dame Edith Evans

529. Julius J. Epstein

530. Robert Enrico

531. George Englund

532. Orson Welles

533. Anita Ekberg

534) What comedian "kicked the bucket" in the opening minutes of *It's A Mad Mad Mad Mad World?*

535) Who portrayed composer Richard Rogers in the 1948 film of *Words and Music?*

536) What zany and creative T.V. comic starred in the comedy films, *Wake Me When It's Over* and *Sail a Crooked Ship?*

537) Who played the Virgin Mary in the 1965 film version of *The Greatest Story Ever Told?*

538) Who played the female lead opposite Ray Bolger in the 1938 musical film entitled *Rosalie?*

539) Who directed the Burt Reynolds football prison drama, *The Longest Yard?*

540) Who played the shy young man in the film of *Tea and Sympathy?*

541) *The Last Detail* starring Jack Nicholson and Randy Quaid was directed by _____ .

542) What well-known choreographer-dancer choreographed the 1953 musical smash version of *The Band Wagon?*

543) Actor George Kennedy portrayed news reporter Lowell Thomas in *Lawrence Of Arabia*. True or False?

. . . Answers

534. Jimmy Durante

535. Tom Drake

536. Ernie Kovacs

537. Dorothy McGuire

538. Eleanor Powell

539. Robert Aldrich

540. John Kerr

541. Hal Ashby

542. Michael Kidd

543. False (Arthur Kennedy)

544) Who won the Best Supporting Actress Oscar for her role in the film of *Zorba the Greek?*

545) The role of the fair Rowena in the 1952 adventure, *Ivanhoe,* was performed by what actress?

546) Mel Brooks portrayed Moses in *History of the World — Part I.* True or False?

547) Who played the role of the babysitter in John Carpenter's *Halloween?*

548) Who played the respectable prostitute in *From Here to Eternity?*

549) What well-known character actor played the part of the Mad Hatter in the 1933 film of *Alice in Wonderland?*

550) What singer-actress played her first dramatic role opposite Richard Widmark in *Death of a Gunfighter?*

551) Who directed the 1970 film version of *The Boys in the Band?*

552) The original musical score for *The Blue Max* was composed by Max Steiner. True or False?

553) Who played the gun-toting lady out to kill John Belushi in *The Blues Brothers?*

. . . Answers

544. Lila Kedrova

545. Joan Fontaine

546. True

547. Jamie Lee Curtis

548. Donna Reed

549. Edward Everett Horton

550. Lena Horne

551. William Friedkin

552. False (Jerry Goldsmith)

553. Carrie Fisher

554) What well-known American actor played the lead in the 1973 Italian comedy, *Alfredo Alfredo?*

555) Who directed the Al Pacino film, entitled *The Panic in Needle Park?*

556) What well-known television star was nominated for a Best Supporting Actor Oscar for his role in *Birdman of Alcatraz?*

557) Who was Albert R. Broccoli's production partner for most of the James Bond films?

558) What actor portrayed George Washington in the 1962 film of *Lafayette?*

559) What screenwriter adapted Allen Drury's best selling novel, *Advise and Consent?*

560) Who directed the 1951 Kirk Douglas film, *Ace in the Hole?*

561) The role of Queen Christina of Sweden in *The Abdication* was performed by what actress?

562) Actor Bill Travers played the title role in *Wee Geordie*. True or False?

563) What black actor directed and produced *Book of Numbers?*

. . . Answers

554. Dustin Hoffman

555. Jerry Schatzberg

556. Telly Savalas

557. Harry Saltzman

558. Howard St. John

559. Wendell Mayes

560. Billy Wilder

561. Liv Ullmann

562. True

563. Raymond St. Jacques

564) The female lead in *Altered States* was played by Carrie Snodgrass. True or False?

565) Who played the role of the Broadway playboy in the 1958 film of Irwin Shaw's *The Young Lions?*

566) The title role in *Young Cassidy* was acted by whom?

567) Who wrote the screenplay for the Beatles' cartoon film, *Yellow Submarine?*

568) The oldest of the three leading roles in Robert Altman's *Three Women* was portrayed by what actress?

569) The farmer father of *The Yearling* was played by actor Robert Taylor. True or False?

570) What actor portrayed the title role in *Fitzcarraldo?*

571) The Academy Award-winning Best Picture, *Chariots of Fire,* was directed by whom?

572) The male lead in *Eyewitness* was played by William Hurt. True or False?

573) Who played the female lead opposite Oliver Reed in Ken Russell's *The Devils?*

574) Who sang the title song to the James Bond Film, *You Only Live Twice?*

. . . *Answers*

564. False (Blair Brown)

565. Dean Martin

566. Rod Taylor

567. Erich Segal

568. Janice Rule

569. False (Gregory Peck)

570. Klaus Kinski

571. Hugh Hudson

572. True

573. Vanessa Redgrave

574. Nancy Sinatra

575) What city served as the background in *The Verdict?*

576) The role of the senior judge in . . . *And Justice for All* was portrayed by what actor?

577) Did Rocky win the fight at the conclusion of *Rocky?*

578) What actor played the part of the mad bomber in *Rollercoaster?*

579) The film *48 Hours,* took place in what city?

580) *Next Stop, Greenwich Village* was written and directed by whom?

581) Actress Susan Anspach played the female lead in *Getting Straight.* True or False?

582) For Mike Nichols's *Carnal Knowledge,* who wrote the original screenplay?

583) What actor portrayed the title character in *The Marriage of a Young Stockbroker?*

584) The Beatles' final film, *Let It Be,* was directed by Michael Wadleigh. True or False?

585) Who directed *Goldfinger?*

586) What actor portrayed the male lead in Hitchcock's *Marnie?*

. . . *Answers*

575. Boston

576. Jack Warner

577. No, but he went the distance

578. Timothy Bottoms

579. San Francisco

580. Paul Mazursky

581. False (Candice Bergen)

582. Jules Feiffer

583. Richard Benjamin

584. False (Michael Lindsay-Hogg)

585. Guy Hamilton

586. Sean Connery

QUESTIONS

587) The female lead in *Coma* was performed by what actress?

588) John Frankenheimer directed the 1976 adventure film entitled *Swashbuckler.* True or False?

589) The role of Dr. Krankeit, in the film version of *Candy,* was played by whom?

590) The leading French race car driver in *Grand Prix* was played by what actor?

591) *Bye Bye Braverman* was directed by Sidney Lumet. True or False?

592) What beauty queen played the female lead in *Our Man Flint?*

593) What actor portrayed Dreyfus in the film, *I Accuse!?*

594) The role of the goldengirl in *Goldfinger* was performed by actress Honor Blackman. True or False?

595) What actress portrayed Paul Muni's sister in the original *Scarface?*

596) Who directed the Frank Sinatra detective film, *Tony Rome?*

. . . Answers

587. Genevieve Bujold

588. False (James Goldstone)

589. James Coburn

590. Yves Montand

591. True

592. Gila Golan

593. Jose Ferrer

594. False (Shirley Eaton)

595. Ann Dvorak

596. Gordon Douglas

QUESTIONS

597) The title role of gangster Louis Buchalter in *Lepke* was played by whom?

598) Who played the male lead in *The Quiller Memorandum?*

599) Who directed Walter Matthau in *Kotch?*

600) The evil assassin in *The Man With the Golden Gun* was portrayed by what actor?

601) Who played the role of Piano Man in *Lady Sings the Blues?*

602) What comic actor was originally cast in the leading role in Billy Wilder's *Kiss Me, Stupid?*

603) Screenwriters Nancy Meyers, Charles Shyer and Harvey Miller wrote what 1980 hit comedy starring Goldie Hawn?

604) What actress was nominated for an Oscar for her performance in *Tom Jones?*

605) In the 1955 film comedy, *The Seven Little Foys,* who made a cameo appearance in the role of George M. Cohan?

606) Who portrayed Sherlock Holmes in the 1978 film version of *The Hound of the Baskervilles?*

. . . *Answers*

597. Tony Curtis

598. George Segal

599. Jack Lemmon

600. Christopher Lee

601. Richard Pryor

602. Peter Sellers

603. *Private Benjamin*

604. Diane Cilento

605. James Cagney

606. Peter Cook

QUESTIONS

607) *Tell Them Willie Boy is Here* was written and directed by whom?

608) What famous composer won an Academy Award for his musical score for *The Heiress?*

609) What child actor portrayed the title role in the 1960 Walt Disney film, *Toby Tyler?*

610) Who played Kirk Douglas's brother in *The Brotherhood?*

611) Who portrayed Leopold Bloom in the 1967 film version of James Joyce's *Ulysses?*

612) What young actress played the part of Tallulah in the musical film, *Bugsy Malone?*

613) In *Pinky,* who played the part of a black girl who passed for white?

614) The original Warner brothers were named Harry, Jack, Sam and _____ .

615) The role of the narrator, Nick Carraway, in the 1974 version of *The Great Gatsby,* was played by Josef Sommer. True or False?

616) *Catch-22* was photographed by what British cinematographer?

. . . *Answers*

607. Abraham Polonsky

608. Aaron Copland

609. Kevin Corcoran

610. Alex Cord

611. Milo O'Shea

612. Jodie Foster

613. Jeanne Crain

614. Albert

615. False (Sam Waterston)

616. David Watkin

617) In *Bullitt,* the role of the corrupt politician was played by what actor?

618) The title role in *The Wizard of Oz* was performed by Dennis Morgan. True or False?

619) Who directed 1976 French production of *Mr. Klein* which starred Alain Delon?

620) Who played the role of the waitress friend of the title character in *Alice Doesn't Live Here Anymore?*

621) The 1950 original Japanese version of *Rashomon* was directed by whom?

622) What Eurasian actress made her film debut in *The World of Suzie Wong?*

623) Who directed John Belushi and Blair Brown in the 1981 film comedy entitled *Continental Divide?*

624) What Dutch-born actress portrayed the title role in *Emmanuelle?*

625) Who portrayed Garp's mother in *The World According to Garp?*

626) What well-known lyricist's life story was told in *I'll See You in My Dreams?*

. . . *Answers*

617. Robert Vaughan

618. False (Frank Morgan)

619. Joseph Losey

620. Diane Ladd

621. Akira Kurosawa

622. Nancy Kwan

623. Michael Apted

624. Sylvia Kristel

625. Glenn Close

626. Gus Kahn

QUESTIONS

627) Name the member of a famous acting family who appeared in *E. T. — The Extra-terrestrial*.

628) Who was the male lead in the 1970 film, *The Landlord?*

629) *The Last Waltz* chronicled the farewell performance of what rock group?

630) Who played the role of Lily Von Shtupp in Mel Brooks's *Blazing Saddles?*

631) What German-born actor portrayed a Nazi U-boat commander in the 1957 war film, *The Enemy Below?*

632) What famous animator helped create Bugs Bunny, Daffy Duck, Tweetie Pie and Road Runner, among others?

633) Who was nominated for a Best Supporting Actress Oscar for her role in *The Bachelor Party?*

634) The 1976 film entitled *Lipstick* presented what model in her film debut?

635) What playwright wrote the original screenplay for *Splendor in the Grass?*

636) Who played the female lead in the 1964 science-fiction adventure, *First Men in the Moon?*

... *Answers*

627. Drew Barrymore

628. Beau Bridges

629. The Band

630. Madeline Kahn

631. Curt Jurgens

632. Chuck Jones

633. Carolyn Jones

634. Margaux Hemingway

635. William Inge

636. Martha Hyer

QUESTIONS

637) Who played Wayne Rogers's leading lady in *Once in Paris?*

638) The male lead in *Trouble Man* was portrayed by what actor?

639) What actor was nominated for a Best Supporting Oscar for his performance as Uncle Chris in the 1948 film version of *I Remember Mama?*

640) In the 1941 film entitled *Two-Faced Woman*, what international star made her last screen appearance?

641) Who directed *Naked City?*

642) What actor directed the 1958 adventure film, *The Buccaneer?*

643) Who produced the film version of *Grease?*

644) Who played the role of Tillie opposite Walter Matthau in *Pete 'n' Tillie?*

645) Who directed *How to Stuff a Wild Bikini?*

646) Who played the title role in the 1956 biography, *The Benny Goodman Story?*

647) *Bonnie and Clyde* and *Dog Day Afternoon* were both edited by _____ .

. . . *Answers*

637. Gayle Hunnicutt

638. Robert Hooks

639. Oscar Homolka

640. Greta Garbo

641. Jules Dassin

642. Anthony Quinn

643. Allan Carr

644. Carol Burnett

645. William Asher

646. Steve Allen

647. Dede Allen

QUESTIONS

648) Claudette Colbert won the Best Actress Oscar for her performance in what 1934 film?

649) What playwright wrote the screenplay for *The Heartbreak Kid?*

650) What actor portrayed the title role in the 1944 film, *The Mask of Dimitrios?*

651) Who played the role of Paxton Quigley in *Three in the Attic?*

652) Who portrayed Clint Eastwood's sidekick in *Thunderbolt and Lightfoot?*

653) Who played the male lead in the 1965 film entitled *The War Lord?*

654) What actor played the title role in *Conrack?*

655) The film version of *The Tin Drum* was directed by whom?

656) Who wrote the screenplay of *Rachel, Rachel?*

657) Who played the female lead opposite Peter Sellers in *I Love You, Alice B. Toklas?*

658) Who produced *Casablanca?*

. . . Answers

648. *It Happened One Night*

649. Neil Simon

650. Zachary Scott

651. Christopher Jones

652. Jeff Bridges

653. Charlton Heston

654. Jon Voight

655. Volker Schlondorff

656. Stewart Stern

657. Leigh Taylor-Young

658. Hal B. Wallis

559) Who played the role of Chang in the 1937 version of *Lost Horizon?*

560) What composer was responsible for the musical scores for both *Sunset Boulevard* and *A Place in the Sun?*

561) What comic actor starred opposite Richard Pryor in *Stir Crazy?*

562) Elliott Gould starred in *Hopscotch* opposite Glenda Jackson. True or False?

563) Who directed *The Apprenticeship of Duddy Kravitz?*

564) What popular American television star played the male lead in *Goodbye My Fancy?*

565) What novelist supplied the script for Hitchcock's *The Birds?*

566) The role of Pope Julius II in *The Agony and the Ecstacy* was played by Claude Rains. True or False?

567) What actor portrayed the hero pilot in *Airplane?*

568) The role of the villain in *Fuzz* was played by what actor?

569) What American city served as the background in *Chinatown?*

. . . Answers

659. H.B. Warner

660. Franz Waxman

661. Gene Wilder

662. False (Walter Matthau)

663. Ted Kotcheff

664. Robert Young

665. Evan Hunter

666. False (Rex Harrison)

667. Robert Hays

668. Yul Brynner

669. Los Angeles

QUESTIONS

670) What actress played the female lead in the musical film, *Chitty Chitty Bang Bang?*

671) Who played the role of General Allenby in *Lawrence of Arabia?*

672) The role of the pleasantly surprised father in *Never Too Late* was performed by what actor?

673) What actor played the part of the cuckolded husband who was murdered in *Body Heat?*

674) Who directed *Mike's Murder?*

675) Who portrayed Eddie Cantor in *The Eddie Cantor Story?*

676) What Swedish actor played the male lead in *Elvira Madigan?*

677) *Around the World in 80 Days* was directed by whom?

678) Who produced the 1949 film, *Portrait of Jennie?*

679) Who played the young lawyer in John Ford's *The Man Who Shot Liberty Valance?*

680) Who composed the musical score to *Chariots of Fire?*

681) What male actor played the lead in *The Thief Who Came to Dinner?*

... Answers

670. Sally Ann Howes

671. Jack Hawkins

672. Paul Ford

673. Richard Crenna

674. James Bridges

675. Keefe Brasselle

676. Thommy Berggren

677. Michael Anderson

678. David O. Selznick

679. James Stewart

680. Vangelis

681. Ryan O'Neal

682) Who portrayed George Segal's mother in *Where's Poppa?*

683) The title character of *Morgan!* was performed by what actor?

684) What playwright wrote the screenplay of *The Misfits?*

685) Who sang the title theme of *To Sir, With Love?*

686) Who directed Clint Eastwood in *The Gauntlet?*

687) Who directed Burt Reynolds in *The End?*

688) The role of the kidnapper in *Experiment in Terror* was played by what actor?

689) In *Diamonds Are Forever,* the role of James Bond was played by Roger Moore. True or False?

690) Who played the sex siren in the film version of *Slaughterhouse Five?*

691) What actress portrayed the title role in *Baby Doll?*

692) Who directed *Lord Love a Duck?*

693) *Quest for Fire* dealt with foot racing in the Olympics. True or False?

. . . *Answers*

682. Ruth Gordon

683. David Warner

684. Arthur Miller

685. Lulu

686. Clint Eastwood

687. Burt Reynolds

688. Ross Martin

689. False (Sean Connery)

690. Valerie Perrine

691. Carroll Baker

692. George Axelrod

693. False (*Chariots of Fire*)

694) The role of the Inca king in *The Royal Hunt of the Sun* was portrayed by what actor?

695) Who directed *Buddy Buddy?*

696) What American actor played the male lead in *Hellcats in the Navy?*

697) Who played the role of Marion Ravenswood in *Raiders of the Lost Ark?*

698) Who appeared in *Close Encounters of the Third Kind*, Teri Carr or Melinda Dillon?

699) Who played the male lead opposite Brooke Shields in *The Blue Lagoon?*

700) *The Four Seasons* was written and directed by whom?

701) Who created the special effects for both *Jason and the Argonauts* and *The Golden Voyage of Sinbad?*

702) The role of H. G. Wells, in *Time After Time,* was portrayed by what actor?

703) Who was the main creator of Paramount Pictures?

704) *The Leopard* was directed by what Italian filmmaker?

. . . *Answers*

694. Christopher Plummer

695. Billy Wilder

696. Ronald Reagan

697. Karen Allen

698. Both

699. Christopher Atkins

700. Alan Alda

701. Ray Harryhausen

702. Malcolm McDowell

703. Adolph Zukor

704. Luchino Visconti

705) Who played the female lead in *Sphinx?*

706) What American actor portrayed Wyatt Earp in *My Darling Clementine?*

707) Who played Lord Epping in *Mexican Spitfire?*

708) What actor starred in the 1950 thriller, *State Secret?*

709) Who wrote, produced and directed *The Victors?*

710) Who composed the original score for *Trouble Man?*

711) The 1962 all-star recreation of D-day 1944 was entitled _____ .

712) What actress played the female lead in *Bunny Lake Is Missing?*

713) Who played the title role in *The Hoodlum Priest?*

714) *What Lola Wants* was the British title for the American film musical entitled _____ .

715) Who played the male lead in the film version of John Steinbeck's *Cannery Row?*

716) *Missing* was written and directed by whom?

717) Who portrayed Charlie, the border patrol guard, in *The Border?*

. . . *Answers*

705. Lesley-Anne Downe

706. Henry Fonda

707. Leon Errol

708. Douglas Fairbanks, Jr.

709. Carl Foreman

710. Marvin Gaye

711. *The Longest Day*

712. Carol Lynley

713. Don Murray

714. *Damn Yankees*

715. Nick Nolte

716. Costa-Gavras

717. Jack Nicholson

718) *Making Love* involved a love affair between two women. True or False?

719) Who played Rigby Reardon in *Dead Men Don't Wear Plaid?*

720) What American actress portrayed Barbara Gordon in *I'm Dancing as Fast as I Can?*

721) *Diner* was written and directed by whom?

722) Who portrayed boxer Clubber Lang in *Rocky III?*

723) Who directed the film version of the musical, *Annie?*

724) E.T., the creature, was created by what designer?

725) Who played Ivan Travalian in *Author! Author!?*

726) The science-fiction thriller, *Blade Runner,* was directed by Steven Spielberg. True or False?

727) Who performed the role of Khan in *Star Trek II: The Wrath of Khan?*

728) What child actress played the role of Carol Anne in *Poltergeist?*

729) Who played Spicoli in *Fast Times at Ridgemont High?*

. . . *Answers*

718. False (two men)

719. Steve Martin

720. Jill Clayburgh

721. Barry Levinson

722. Mr. T.

723. John Huston

724. Carlo Rambaldi

725. Al Pacino

726. False (Ridley Scott)

727. Ricardo Montalban

728. Heather O'Rourke

729. Sean Penn

QUESTIONS

730) Who played Tex's brother in *Tex?*

731) Who performed the role of Richard Gere's male buddy in *An Officer and a Gentleman?*

732) Where do Ingrid Bergman and Paul Henreid fly off to at the end of *Casablanca?*

733) Who directed *Grease II?*

734) Who played the young male co-star with Clint Eastwood in *Honkytonk Man?*

735) What actor performed the role of Stingo in the film version of William Styron's *Sophie's Choice?*

736) The role of Irena Gallier, in the remake of *Cat People,* was played by whom?

737) What actress played the female lead in *Swamp Thing?*

738) *Megaforce* was directed by what former stunt man?

739) Who portrayed Willie Nelson's sidekick in the western, *Barbarosa?*

740) What actor played the title role in *Monsignor?*

741) In *I, The Jury,* the role of Mike Hammer was portrayed by whom?

. . . Answers

730. Jim Metzler

731. David Keith

732. Lisbon, Portugal

733. Patricia Birch

734. Kyle Eastwood, Clint's son

735. Peter MacNicol

736. Natassia Kinski

737. Adrienne Barbeau

738. Hal Needham

739. Gary Busey

740. Christopher Reeve

741. Armand Assante

QUESTIONS

742) Who directed Stephen King's screenplay for *Creepshow?*

743) The hit Brazilian film, *Dona Flor and Her Two Husbands,* was remade with an American background and entitled _____ .

744) What actress played the leading role of the mother in *Six Weeks?*

745) Who won the 1982 Academy Award for Best Supporting Actress?

746) What Australian actor played Max in *The Road Warrior?*

747) *Diva* was co-written and directed by whom?

748) The role of the elder rabbi, in *The Chosen,* was portrayed by whom?

749) *Moonlighting* starred what British actor?

750) What comic actor played the title role in *The Missionary?*

751) What French director wrote and directed *Bolero?*

752) *Murder, My Sweet* was remade in 1975 as _____ .

753) Who directed *Dr. Terror's House of Horrors?*

. . . *Answers*

742. George A. Romero

743. *Kiss Me Goodbye*

744. Mary Tyler Moore

745. Jessica Lange

746. Mel Gibson

747. Jean-Jacques Beineix

748. Rod Steiger

749. Jeremy Irons

750. Michael Palin

751. Claude Lelouch

752. *Farewell, My Lovely*

753. Freddie Francis

754) Who co-starred with Elliott Gould in *Busting?*

755) *Arrividerci, Baby* starred what actor as the money-hungry fortune hunter.

756) What was the title of the film that chronicled the 1970 U.S. tour of rock stars Joe Cocker and Leon Russell?

757) *My Favorite Spy* starred what actor-comedian opposite Hedy Lamarr?

758) Who wrote the screenplay for *The Great Waldo Pepper?*

759) What famous British model was cast in a starring role in *Privilege?*

760) Who portrayed Buffalo Bill Cody in Robert Altman's *Buffalo Bill and the Indians?*

761) Who directed the film version of *Valley of the Dolls?*

762) Who played the role of the black runaway slave in *The Scalphunters?*

763) *Tickle Me* starred what singing star in the role of a rodeo star?

764) What actor portrayed Hank Williams in the film version of *Your Cheatin' Heart?*

. . . *Answers*

754. Robert Blake

755. Tony Curtis

756. *Mad Dogs and Englishmen*

757. Bob Hope

758. William Goldman

759. Jean Shrimpton

760. Paul Newman

761. Mark Robson

762. Ossie Davis

763. Elvis Presley

764. George Hamilton

QUESTIONS

765) Who performed the role of Sissy Spacek's mother in *Carrie?*

766) James Bond was played by what actor in *On Her Majesty's Secret Service?*

767) Who played the male lead in *Champagne for Caesar?*

768) Who directed *The Formula* which starred Marlon Brando and George C. Scott?

769) What 1970 American film re-created the bombing of Pearl Harbor?

770) Who played Sharkey in *Sharkey's Machine?*

771) What actress portrayed Jack Lord's cheating wife in *God's Little Acre?*

772) Who played the male lead opposite Debbie Reynolds in *Divorce, American Style?*

773) Who directed *The League of Gentlemen?*

774) What child actress portrayed the title role in *The Bad Seed?*

775) Who played Santa Claus in the 1947 version of *Miracle on 34th Street?*

776) Who directed *Friendly Persuasion?*

. . . *Answers*

765. Piper Laurie

766. George Lazenby

767. Ronald Colman

768. John G. Avildsen

769. *Tora! Tora! Tora!*

770. Burt Reynolds

771. Tina Louise

772. Dick Van Dyke

773. Basil Dearden

774. Patty McCormack

775. Edmund Gwenn

776. William Wyler

777) What actor portrayed the young screenwriter in *Sunset Boulevard?*

778) What singer-composer sang the title song to the James Bond film, *The Spy Who Loved Me?*

779) What actor portrayed "Doc" Holliday in *Hour of the Gun?*

780) Who played the role of Loretta Lynn's husband in *Coal Miner's Daughter?*

781) Who wrote the screenplay for *Seven Days in May?*

782) *El Cid* was directed by William Wyler. True or False?

783) Who played the female lead opposite Peter Sellers in *The Bobo?*

784) Who portrayed Jake La Motta's brother, Joey, in *Raging Bull?*

785) Who played the part of Saul Kaplan in *An Unmarried Woman?*

786) Who wrote and directed *White Line Fever?*

787) Who portrayed the title role in the film version of *Luther?*

788) *The Heart Is a Lonely Hunter* was directed by whom?

. . . *Answers*

777. William Holden

778. Carly Simon

779. Jason Robards

780. Tommy Lee Jones

781. Rod Serling

782. False (Anthony Mann)

783. Britt Eckland

784. Joe Pesci

785. Alan Bates

786. Jonathan Kaplan

787. Stacy Keach

788. Robert Ellis Miller

789) Who portrayed James Garner's henchman in *Victor/Victoria?*

790) Who played the role of Miss Mona in the film version of *The Best Little Whorehouse in Texas?*

791) What dress designer married Gene Tierney and almost married Grace Kelly?

792) Who portrayed Jack Cates in *48 Hours?*

793) The role of agent, George Fields, in *Tootsie,* was played by whom?

794) The film version of *The World According to Garp* was directed by George Roy Hill. True or False?

795) Who played the role of Richard Pryor's army buddy in *Some Kind of Hero?*

796) Who portrayed Bathsheba in *David and Bathsheba?*

797) Who played gangster Joey Gallo in *Crazy Joe?*

798) Who directed *The Arrangement?*

799) Author Truman Capote penned the screenplay to *Beat the Devil.* True or False?

800) Who played the title role in *Watermelon Man.*

. . . Answers

789. Alex Karras

790. Dolly Parton

791. Oleg Cassini

792. Nick Nolte

793. Sydney Pollack

794. True

795. Ray Sharkey

796. Susan Hayward

797. Peter Boyle

798. Elia Kazan

799. True

800. Godfrey Cambridge

QUESTIONS

801) What actor portrayed the male lead in the 1958 horror film, *The Blob?*

802) Who directed the 1975 science-fiction thriller, *Rollerball?*

803) What actress played the female lead opposite Gregory Peck in *The Stalking Moon?*

804) The film of the novel, *Hotel,* was directed by whom?

805) What male actor starred in *The Crawling Eye?*

806) The 1960 film version of *The Lost World,* starring Michael Rennie, was directed by disaster-master _____ .

807) What screen actress played the role of Sarah in the film of *The Bible?*

808) What was the name of the talking mule who starred in several film comedies of the 1950s?

809) Who composed the musical score for *Exodus?*

810) The star of Antonioni's *Blow-Up* was David Hemmings. True or False?

811) Zeppo Marx's real first name was _____ .

. . . Answers

801. Steve McQueen

802. Norman Jewison

803. Eva Marie Saint

804. Richard Quine

805. Forrest Tucker

806. Irwin Allen

807. Ava Gardner

808. Francis

809. Ernest Gold

810. True

811. Herbert

QUESTIONS

812) *The Parallax View* starring Warren Beatty was produced and directed by whom?

813) Who played the female lead opposite Steve Martin in *The Jerk?*

814) What actor portrayed *Topper* in films?

815) Who directed *Old Yeller?*

816) *Renaldo and Clara* was written and directed by singer-composer Pete Seeger. True or False?

817) What actor portrayed the part of Roberta Muldoon in the film version of *The World According to Garp?*

818) What playwright also directed the film of *That Championship Season?*

819) What famous model played the target of Bruce Dern's affections in *Tattoo?*

820) What actress portrayed the female lead as a half-breed opposite Burt Lancaster in *The Unforgiven?*

821) What well-known television host directed a film entitled *What Do You Say to a Naked Lady?*

. . . Answers

812. Alan J. Pakula

813. Bernadette Peters

814. Roland Young

815. Robert Stevenson

816. False (Bob Dylan)

817. John Lithgow

818. Jason Miller

819. Maud Adams

820. Audrey Hepburn

821. Allen Funt

822) The film version of *Babes in Arms* was directed by . . .

    a. Hal Roach
    b. George Cukor
    c. George Abbott
    d. Busby Berkeley
    e. Ken Russell

823) Comedian Buddy Hackett had a supporting role in the film version of *The Music Man*. True or False?

824) Who was Gene Wilder's female co-star in *Hanky Panky?*

825) What Harvard-educated filmmaker produced and directed a documentary entitled *Point of Order!* which was based upon the McCarthy hearings?

826) Angie Dickinson, Carroll O'Connor and Lee Marvin were out to kill each other in . . .

    a. *Point Blank*   d. *The Quiller Memorandum*
    b. *Prime Cut*   e. *Law and Order*
    c. *The Professionals*

824) In the 1934 screen version of *Treasure Island*, the
827) Twiggy and Tommy Tune danced together in Ken Russell's film version of *The Boy Friend*. True or False?

828) Who played the male lead in *Grease 2?*

829) What famous novelist wrote the screenplay for *Gunfight at the O.K. Corral?*

. . . *Answers*

822. (d)

823. True

824. Gilda Radner

825. Emile De Antonio

826. (a)

827. True

828. Maxwell Caulfield

829. Leon Uris

830) Gypsy Rose Lee's mother in the film version of *Gypsy* was played by . . .
    a. Ethel Merman
    b. Martha Raye
    c. Rosalind Russell
    d. Thelma Ritter
    e. Lucille Ball

831) Actress Jean Hagen jumped out of a cake in *Singin' in the Rain*. True or False?

832) What actor portrayed the legendary painter in *El Greco?*

833) What German actor portrayed the title role in *Goldfinger?*

834) *The Singing Nun* was played by Julie Andrews. True or False?

835) Who performed the central role of Sidney Bruhl in the screen version of *Deathtrap?*

836) In the 1934 screen version of *Treasure Island*, the role of Long John Silver was played by whom?

837) Ruth Gordon falls to her death in *Rosemary's Baby*. True or False?

. . . *Answers*

830. (c)

831. False (Debbie Reynolds)

832. Mel Ferrer

833. Gert Frobe

834. False (Debbie Reynolds)

835. Michael Caine

836. Wallace Beery

837. False

838) In *Bonnie and Clyde,* Warren Beatty's older brother was portrayed by . . .

    a. Michael J. Pollard

    b. Gene Hackman

    c. Jack Warden

    d. Ernest Borgnine

    e. David Janssen

839) Who played the role of Apollo Creed in the *Rocky* trilogy?

840) Who played Juliet in Zeffirelli's *Romeo and Juliet?*

841) Howard Keel played the male lead in the screen version of *Annie Get Your Gun.* True or False?

842) Who portrayed the role of J. Edgar Hoover in the 1978 film of *The Brink's Job?*

843) In *Looking For Mr. Goodbar,* Diane Keaton was murdered by . . .

    a. Richard Gere

    b. Richard Attenborough

    c. Steven Bauer

    d. Albert Finney

    e. Tom Berenger

844) Both William Holden and Ernest Borgnine died in the final shootout in *The Wild Bunch.* True or False?

845) What actor did Humphrey Bogart name one of his children after?

. . . *Answers*

838. (b)

839. Carl Weathers

840. Olivia Hussey

841. True

842. Sheldon Leonard

843. (e)

844. True

845. Leslie Howard

846) What actress played the title role in *Lilith?*

847) The title role in Roger Corman's *Machine Gun Kelly* was played by . . .
    a. Richard Dreyfuss
    b. Aldo Ray
    c. Earl Holliman
    d. John Cassavetes
    e. Charles Bronson

848) Who played the role of the teenage son in *Max Dugan Returns?*

849) Who played the title role in the 1957 film comedy, *The Sad Sack?*

850) Clint Eastwood's Dirty Harry is murdered at the conclusion of *Sudden Impact*. True or False?

851) What actor portrayed Sam Houston in *The Alamo?*

852) Who directed both *The War of the Worlds* and *Robinson Crusoe on Mars?*

853) The role of the dwarf in *Ship of Fools* was played by whom?

854) Dustin Hoffman turned killer in . . .
    a. *The Getaway*   d. *Straw Dogs*
    b. *Kramer vs. Kramer*   e. *The Godfather*
    c. *Marathon Man*

. . . *Answers*

846. Jean Seberg

847. (e)

848. Matthew Broderick

849. Jerry Lewis

850. False

851. Richard Boone

852. Byron Haskin

853. Michael Dunn

854. (d)

855) Who portrayed the evil Thulsa Doom in *Conan the Barbarian?*

856) Who portrayed the female lead in Roman Polanski's *Repulsion?*

857) The music for the widely acclaimed film, *The Umbrellas of Cherbourg,* was composed by . . .
   a. Michel Legrand
   b. Francis Lai
   c. Jacques Demy
   d. Marvin Hamlisch
   e. Gilbert Becaud

858) Audrey Hepburn did her own singing in *My Fair Lady.* True or False?

859) Who played the part of Jean Harlow's agent in the Joseph E. Levine-produced screen biography, entitled *Harlow?*

860) The strolling balladeers of *Cat Ballou* were Nat King Cole and _____ .

861) Who portrayed Ulrich the sorcerer in *Dragonslayer?*

862) Who played the title role in *The Exorcist?*

863) Who portrayed Willy Loman in the screen version of Arthur Miller's *Death of a Salesman?*

. . . Answers

855. James Earl Jones

856. Catherine Deneuve

857. (a)

858. False (Marnie Nixon sang for her)

859. Red Buttons

860. Stubby Kaye

861. Ralph Richardson

862. Max von Sydow

863. Frederic March

864) Laurence Olivier kills Roy Scheider midway through *Marathon Man*. True or False?

865) What opera star played the title role in *Yes, Giorgio?*

866) What Italian composer scored almost all of Fellini's films?

867) What actor portrayed the master of ceremonies in *They Shoot Horses, Don't They?*

868) The assassin in *The Day of the Jackal* was played by . . .

    a. James Fox
    b. Gregory Peck
    c. Ralph Meeker
    d. Rutger Hauer
    e. Edward Fox

869) Michael Caine murdered practically the entire cast in *The Island*. True or False?

870) *Scent of Mystery* was the only film produced which utilized a process named _____ .

871) Who wrote, dubbed and edited *What's Up, Tiger Lily?*

872) What actress played the female lead opposite Frederic Forrest in *Hammett?*

. . . *Answers*

864. True

865. Luciano Pavarotti

866. Nino Rota

867. Gig Young

868. (e)

869. True

870. Smell-o-vision

871. Woody Allen

872. Marilu Henner

873) What screenwriter won the Oscar for Best Screenplay for *From Here to Eternity?*

874) Zero Mostel played Tevye in the film of *Fiddler on the Roof.* True or False?

875) This young actor portrayed the psychopathic killer in *Dirty Harry.* Who is it?
    a. James Woods
    b. Raul Julia
    c. Andy Robinson
    d. Richard Widmark
    e. Tom Berenger

876) Who portrayed Johnnie Smith in the screen version of Stephen King's *The Dead Zone?*

877) What actress played the female lead in *Endangered Species?*

878) The role of Alex's girlfriend in *The Big Chill* was performed by whom?

879) *A Hard Day's Night* and *Help!* were both directed by George Martin. True or False?

880) What actor played the part of a motorcycle cop in Francis Coppola's *The Rain People?*

. . . Answers

873. Daniel Taradash

874. False (Topol)

875. (c)

876. Christopher Walken

877. JoBeth Williams

878. Meg Tilly

879. False (Richard Lester)

880. Robert Duvall

881) Actor Robert Walker portrayed this composer in *Till the Clouds Roll By* . . .

    a. George Gershwin
    b. Lorenz Hart
    c. Cole Porter
    d. Oscar Hammerstein II
    e. Jerome Kern

882) Who directed *Heaven's Gate?*

883) Tippi Hedren murders Suzanne Pleshette in Hitchcock's *The Birds*. True or False?

884) What Italian actor played the title role in the James Bond film, *Thunderball?*

885) Who wrote the screenplay for *Midnight Express?*

886) Who played the title role in *The Rise and Fall of Legs Diamond?*

    a. Warren Oates
    b. Robert Conrad
    c. Vic Morrow
    d. Ray Danton
    e. Jason Robards

887) What female director was responsible for *The Night Porter?*

888) What rock star played the title role in *McVicar?*

. . . Answers

881. (e)

882. Michael Cimino

883. False

884. Adolfo Celi

885. Oliver Stone

886. (d)

887. Liliana Cavani

888. Roger Daltrey

889) Actor Alan Bates played the role of Bill Sykes in the musical film of *Oliver?* True or False?

890) What British actor played the role of the decadent valet in *The Servant?*

891) Al Pacino's Michael Corleone dies at the conclusion of *Godfather II*. True or False?

892) Hitchcock's *Psycho* was based upon the novel by whom?

893) The lyrics to the music of the film of *Roberta* were written by . . .
   a. Jerome Kern
   b. Ira Gershwin
   c. Oscar Hammerstein II
   d. Cole Porter
   e. Adolph Green

894) Who played the role of Dolly Levi in the screen version of *The Matchmaker?*

895) Who portrayed Billie Burke in *The Great Ziegfeld?*

896) Julie Andrews did her own singing in *Mary Poppins*. True or False?

897) Who directed Richard Burton and Elizabeth Taylor in *The Sandpiper?*

898) *Intolerance* was directed by what silent filmmaker?

. . . Answers

889. False (Oliver Reed)

890. Dirk Bogarde

891. False

892. Robert Bloch

893. (c)

894. Shirley Booth

895. Myrna Loy

896. True

897. Vincente Minnelli

898. D.W. Griffith

899) The male lead in *Romancing the Stone* was played by whom?

900) James Mason's henchman in Hitchcock's *North by Northwest* was . . .
    a. Martin Balsam
    b. Martin Landau
    c. Martin Miller
    d. Martin Sheen
    e. Cary Grant

901) Fay Dunaway and Jack Nicholson walk off together at the conclusion of *Chinatown*. True or False?

902) Who played the title role in the James Bond adventure, *Dr. No?*

903) In the 1975 version of *Capone,* gangster Al Capone was played by . . .
    a. Rod Steiger
    b. Ben Gazzara
    c. John Cassavetes
    d. Peter Falk
    e. Peter Boyle

904) In the same film, hit man Frank Nittie was portrayed by . . .
    a. George Segal
    b. Kris Kristofferson
    c. Al Pacino
    d. Peter Boyle
    e. Sylvester Stallone

. . . Answers

899. Michael Douglas

900. (b)

901. False (Dunaway is killed)

902. Joseph Wiseman

903. (b)

904. (e)

905) In Terrence Malick's *Badlands,* the murderers on the run were Sissy Spacek and Warren Oates. True or False?

906) Who wrote, directed and produced *Benji?*

907) What actor starred as a student radical in the film version of *The Strawberry Statement?*

908) What French director was responsible for *Children of Paradise?*

909) Popeye Doyle gets his revenge in *The French Connection* by shooting Charnier. True or False?

910) Who played Fatima Blush in *Never Say Never Again?*

911) Who wrote the screenplay and directed the film version of *The Right Stuff?*

912) Dean Martin had a starring role in . . .
    a. *Bell, Book and Candle*
    b. *Pal Joey*
    c. *Bells Are Ringing*
    d. *The Pajama Game*
    e. *Damn Yankees*

913) What actor played the title role in *Hans Christian Andersen?*

914) *Escape from New York* was directed by whom?

...Answers

905. False (Martin Sheen)

906. Joe Camp

907. Bruce Davison

908. Marcel Carne

909. False (*French Connection II*)

910. Barbara Carrera

911. Phil Kaufman

912. (c)

913. Danny Kaye

914. John Carpenter

915) What actress played the role of the newspaper reporter in *Strange Invaders?*

916) What movie star turned "Rudolph the Red-Nosed Reindeer" into a hit record?

917) Who directed *Flashdance?*

918) Who composed the musical score to *Raiders of the Lost Ark?*

919) Who portrayed the title role in the screen biography of *Freud?*

920) *Terms of Endearment* was written for the screen and directed by _____ .

921) In *The Girl in the Red Velvet Swing,* architect Stanford White was shot and killed by millionaire Harry K. Thaw. Who played the role of Thaw?
    a. Robert Walker
    b. Farley Granger
    c. Rod Taylor
    d. John Forsythe
    e. Anton Diffring

922) In Brian De Palma's *Dressed to Kill,* what actress was brutally slain during the first part of the film?

. . . *Answers*

915. Nancy Allen

916. Gene Autry

917. Adrian Lyne

918. John Williams

919. Montgomery Clift

920. James L. Brooks

921. (b)

922. Angie Dickinson

923) Only two films in the history of the Academy Awards have ever won awards for best picture, best actor and best actress. One of the acclaimed films was *It Happened One Night*. What was the other?

924) Who directed *The Running Man*, which starred Laurence Harvey?

925) What British actor portrayed "M" in many of the James Bond films?

926) Who played the female lead in the film version of *Up the Down Staircase?*

927) _____ and David DePatie created the cartoon character of the Pink Panther.

928) What actress provided the off-screen voice of the demon for the *The Exorcist?*

929) Who portrayed the male lead in *Prince of the City?*

930) *Brigadoon* took place in Ireland. True or False?

931) What French entertainer played the role of the piano player in the Truffaut film entitled *Shoot the Piano Player?*

932) Who directed the film of *The Spy Who Came in From the Cold?*

933) Who portrayed John F. Kennedy in *P.T.-109?*

... *Answers*

923. *One Flew Over the Cuckoo's Nest*

924. Sir Carol Reed

925. Bernard Lee

926. Sandy Dennis

927. Friz Freleng

928. Mercedes McCambridge

929. Treat Williams

930. False (Scotland)

931. Charles Aznavour

932. Martin Ritt

933. Cliff Robertson

QUESTIONS

934) Who played the role of Polly Benedict, Andy Hardy's faithful girlfriend in the Andy Hardy series?

935) *Seven Beauties* was written and directed by Federico Fellini. True or False?

936) Who played the title role in *The Front?*

937) Who portrayed astronaut Bowman in *2001: A Space Odyssey?*

938) What French actor played the lead role in *Z?*

939) Who played Richard of Gloucester in *Tower of London?*
   a. Peter Lorre
   b. Peter Cushing
   c. Christopher Lee
   d. Boris Karloff
   e. Vincent Price

940) Who produced and directed *Therese and Isabelle?*

941) Who portrayed Admiral Halsey in *The Gallant Hours?*

942) What was the sequel to *My Friend Flicka?*

943) What singer-songwriter played a dramatic female lead in the 1953 version of *The Jazz Singer?*

... Answers

934. Ann Rutherford

935. False (Lina Wertmuller)

936. Woody Allen

937. Keir Dullea

938. Yves Montand

939. (e)

940. Radley Metzger

941. James Cagney

942. *Green Grass of Wyoming*

943. Peggy Lee

QUESTIONS

944) Who played the role of Garp's wife in the film version of *The World According to Garp?*

945) Who played Raskolnikov in the 1935 film of *Crime and Punishment?*
   a. Boris Karloff
   b. Laurence Olivier
   c. Ralph Richardson
   d. Peter Lorre
   e. Vincent Price

946) Who plays the role of Luke Skywalker in the *Star Wars* trilogy?

947) Nick Nolte's co-star in *North Dallas Forty* was singer _____ .

948) Lana Lang was portrayed by Annette O'Toole in *Superman III*. True or False?

949) In *Dillinger,* Melvin Purvis was played by . . .
   a. Warren Oates
   b. Robert De Niro
   c. Robert Conrad
   d. Don Johnson
   e. Ben Johnson

950) Who had the female lead in the 1960 film version of *The Time Machine?*

951) What was the title of the 1955 film which starred Richard Burton in the role of actor Edwin Booth?

. . . Answers

944. Mary Beth Hurt

945. (d)

946. Mark Hamill

947. Mac Davis

948. True

949. (e)

950. Yvette Mimieux

951. *Prince of Players*

QUESTIONS

952) What comedian played the title role in the 1948 film entitled *The Fuller Brush Man?*

953) Country singer Patsy Cline was played by what actress in *Coal Miner's Daughter?*

954) Both versions of *Where the Boys Are* take place in what American town?

955) *The Priest of Love* is the film biography of what famous novelist?

956) Who is the president of the Motion Picture Association of America?

957) Who portrayed the title role in *The Gene Krupa Story?*

958) *Invitation to the Dance* was directed and choreographed by whom?

959) What actor played the role of John Wayne's adopted son in *Red River?*

960) Who played the male lead in Walt Disney's film version of *Babes in Toyland?*

. . . Answers

952. Red Skelton

953. Beverly D'Angelo

954. Fort Lauderdale, Florida

955. D.H. Lawrence

956. Jack Valenti

957. Sal Mineo

958. Gene Kelly

959. Montgomery Clift

960. Tommy Sands

961) Who murdered Richard Widmark in Agatha Christie's *Murder on the Orient Express?*
    a. Peter Finch
    b. Mia Farrow
    c. practically the entire cast
    d. Donald Sutherland
    e. Tony Musante

962) Who directed the film version of Gore Vidal's *Myra Breckinridge?*

963) What comic actor portrayed Hitler in Mel Brooks's *The Producers?*

964) Lily Tomlin's husband in *The Incredible Shrinking Woman* was played by whom?

965) Actress Janet Leigh had a role in John Carpenter's *The Fog.* True or False?

966) What well-known male actor gave his first screen performance in the 1946 version of *The Killers?*
    a. Edmond O'Brien
    b. Ernest Borgnine
    c. James Coburn
    d. Burt Lancaster
    e. Kirk Douglas

967) What actor saved Fay Wray from the clutches of King Kong?

. . . Answers

961. (c)

962. Michael Sarne

963. Dick Shawn

964. Charles Grodin

965. True

966. (d)

967. Bruce Cabot

QUESTIONS

968) The role of Arkady in the screen version of *Gorky Park* was played by whom?

969) Who directed *Blindfold,* the 1966 suspense thriller starring Rock Hudson?

970) Who played the title role in *Alvarez Kelly?*

971) What actress portrayed Willy Loman's wife in both the stage and screen versions of *Death of a Salesman?*

972) Who played Napoleon in the 1956 film of *War and Peace?*

973) The 1979 Sherlock Holmes mystery, *Murder by Decree,* involves . . .
   a. Jack the Ripper
   b. the murder of the King of England
   c. the kidnapping of Queen Victoria
   d. Winston Churchill's parents
   e. an attempt on Abraham Lincoln's life

974) The title role in *Tarzan the Magnificent* (1960) was played by whom?

975) What actress portrayed James Dean's mother in *East of Eden?*

976) Who starred in and directed *The Naked Prey?*

977) *Against All Odds* is a remake of what film noir classic?

. . . Answers

968. William Hurt

969. Philip Dunne

970. William Holden

971. Mildred Dunnock

972. Herbert Lom

973. (a)

974. Gordon Scott

975. Jo Van Fleet

976. Cornel Wilde

977. *Out of the Past*

978) Oscar-winner Jack Nicholson portrayed astronaut _____ in *Terms of Endearment*.

979) Daria Halprin and _____ starred in Antonioni's *Zabriskie Point*.

980) Who plays the role of Goldie Hawn's husband in *Swing Shift?*

981) *Four for Texas* starred Frank Sinatra, Dean Martin, Ursula Andress and Anita Ekberg. True or False?

982) Who composed the original musical score for *The Right Stuff?*

983) What playwright's life was told in the screen version of *Act One?*

984) Who played the role of the blind girl in *A Patch of Blue?*

985) Six-month-old _____ played opposite Maurice Chevalier in *Bedtime Story*.

986) The murderous robot in *Westworld* was actually actor . . .
   a. Richard Benjamin
   b. Richard Boone
   c. Yul Brynner
   d. Kirk Douglas
   e. Lee Marvin

. . . Answers

978. Garrett Breedlove

979. Mark Frechette

980. Ed Harris

981. True

982. Bill Conti

983. Moss Hart

984. Elizabeth Hartman

985. Baby LeRoy

986. (c)

QUESTIONS

987) Both *The Shooting* and *Ride in the Whirlwind* were directed by whom?

988) What was the name of the child actress who played the romantic female lead opposite Carl "Alfalfa" Switzer in the Our Gang comedies?

989) Who played the role of Gypo Nolan in John Ford's *The Informer?*

990) What actor performed his last role in the film version of *The Last Angry Man?*

991) Paul Williams and _____ played the oddly matched Texas millionaires who commissioned Burt Reynolds to haul beer in *Smokey and the Bandit.*

992) What actor portrayed the role of Barbara Streisand's father in *Yentl?*

993) Who directed *Harper,* starring Paul Newman?

994) What actor played seven roles in *No Way to Treat a Lady?*

995) Who portrayed the village idiot in *Ryan's Daughter?*

. . . Answers

987. Monte Hellman

988. Darla Hood

989. Victor McLaglen

990. Paul Muni

991. Pat McCormick

992. Nehemiah Persoff

993. Jack Smight

994. Rod Steiger

995. John Mills

996) The aging gangster who comes out of retirement in *The Last Run* was played by . . .
   a. George C. Scott
   b. Richard Conte
   c. Frank Sinatra
   d. Tony Curtis
   e. Steve McQueen

997) Actress Shirley MacLaine played opposite Albert Finney in *Charlie Bubbles*. True or False?

998) What actor portrayed Scarlett O'Hara's father in *Gone With The Wind?*

999) What actor gave Shirley Temple her first screen kiss in *Miss Annie Rooney?*

1000) What was the first full-length feature film ever made in Cinerama?

1001) Who directed the 1965 film, *None But the Brave,* which starred Frank Sinatra?

1002) What actor played the role of the warden in *Escape From Alcatraz?*

. . . Answers

996. (a)

997. False (Liza Minelli)

998. Thomas Mitchell

999. Dickie Moore

1000. *The Wonderful World of the Brothers Grimm*

1001. Frank Sinatra

1002. Patrick McGoohan

1003) The two thugs in *The Night of the Following Day* were portrayed by . . .

    a. Eli Wallach and John Cassavetes
    b. Eli Wallach and Keir Dullea
    c. Strother Martin and L.Q. Jones
    d. Robert Duvall and James Caan
    e. Marlon Brando and Richard Boone

1004) Adrienne Barbeau had a supporting role in *Escape From New York.* True or False?

1005) Who directed the film version of *The Dresser?*

1006) Who produced and directed the 1930 film version of *Hell's Angels,* which launched the film career of Jean Harlow?

1007) What actress co-starred with Bill Travers is *Born Free?*

1008) What film pioneer founded Universal Pictures in 1912?

1009) Who played the female lead in *True Grit?*

1010) Who portrayed the title role in the 1934 version of *Cleopatra?*

1011) Who performed the role of Pat Boone's mother in the 1962 film of *State Fair.*

. . . Answers

1003. (e)

1004. True

1005. Peter Yates

1006. Howard Hughes

1007. Virginia McKenna

1008. Carl Laemmle

1009. Kim Darby

1010. Claudette Colbert

1011. Alice Faye

1012) What comic actor's trademark is a popping sound made by slapping a hand to his open mouth?

1013) Who directed *Sweet Smell of Success,* which starred Burt Lancaster and Tony Curtis?

1014) The role of Connie Corleone in the *Godfather* films was played by whom?

1015) Who directed the 1943 film version of *Watch on the Rhine?*

1016) What production executive was hailed as "The Boy Wonder" during the 1920s and 1930s?

1017) Who played the title role in the film version of *Candy?*

1018) Who portrayed the title role in *Dr. Cyclops?*

1019) What actress starred opposite Peter O'Toole in *Murphy's War?*

1020) Actress Penny Marshall played the role of Errol Flynn's love interest in *The Sea Hawk* (1940). True or False?

1021) Who produced *California Suite?*

1022) What actor played the role of the devil in the screen version of *Damn Yankees?*

. . . Answers

1012. Fritz Feld

1013. Alexander Mackendrick

1014. Talia Shire

1015. Herman Shumlin

1016. Irving G. Thalberg

1017. Ewa Aulin

1018. Albert Dekker

1019. Sian Philips

1020. False (Brenda Marshall)

1021. Ray Stark

1022. Ray Walston

1023) What actress played the role of Elliott's mother in *E. T. — The Extra-terrestrial?*

1024) What 1935 film made Errol Flynn an international star?

1025) Who was the female star of Woody Allen's *Bananas?*

1026) In what 1930s movie was the following line uttered: "It was beauty that killed the beast"?

1027) How many times has Hollywood filmed Dashiell Hammett's novel, *The Maltese Falcon?*

1028) In what movie did Marlon Brando sing and dance?

1029) In what movie did Greta Garbo play a communist?

. . . Answers

1023. Dee Wallace

1024. *Captain Blood*

1025. Louis Lasser

1026. *King Kong*

1027. Three

1028. *Guys and Dolls*

1029. *Ninotchka*

THE SURVIVALIST SERIES
by Jerry Ahern